LIGHTHOUSES

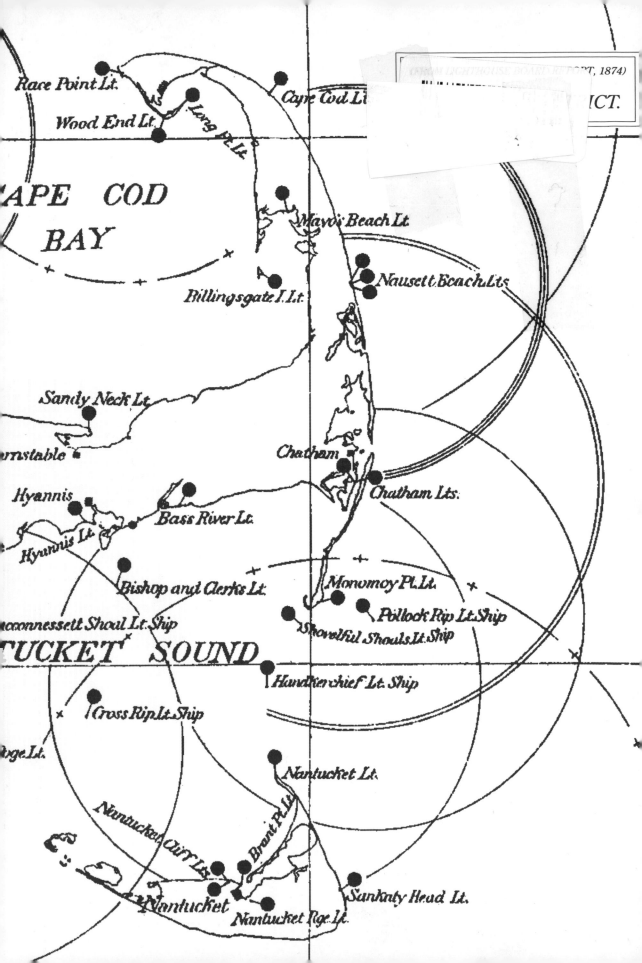

Race Point Lt.

Wood End Lt.

Long Pt. Lt.

Cape Cod Lt.

(FROM LIGHTHOUSE BOARD REPORT, 1874)

DISTRICT.

CAPE COD
BAY

Mayo's Beach Lt.

Nausett Beach Lts.

Billingsgate I. Lt.

Sandy Neck Lt.

Barnstable

Chatham

Chatham Lts.

Hyannis

Bass River Lt.

Hyannis Lt.

Bishop and Clerks Lt.

Monomoy Pt. Lt.

Pollock Rip Lt. Ship

Succonnessett Shoal Lt. Ship

Shovelful Shoals Lt. Ship

NANTUCKET SOUND

Handkerchief Lt. Ship

Cross Rip Lt. Ship

Edge Lt.

Nantucket Lt.

Nantucket Cliff Lts.

Brant Pt. Lt.

Sankaty Head Lt.

Nantucket

Nantucket Bge. Lt.

LIGHTHOUSES

of

Cape Cod—Martha's Vineyard—Nantucket

Their History and Lore

Admont G. Clark
Captain USCGR, Retired

![PI logo]

PARNASSUS IMPRINTS
East Orleans, Massachusetts

ISBN 0-940160-54-4

Library of Congress Catalog Card Number   91-068256

For my wife Ruth, whose humor outlasted the ordeal . . .

Contents

But First a Word . . .

*F*rom my house in Dennis on any clear night I can see the flash of Highland Light, nineteen miles away across Cape Cod Bay. It is a comforting sight. There have been many dark nights on the wide waters of the world when such a light has told me just where I was.

All those who go "in peril on the seas" have owed their lives to the men and women who faithfully tended the lights. So important was this duty that at least down to the Civil War keepers' commissions were signed by the President. In 1806 Thomas Jefferson wrote: "I think the keepers of lighthouses should be dismissed for small degrees of remissness, because of the calamities which even these produce . . ."

The open seas are no problem. You have a pretty good idea of where you are from the sun and stars. But when shorelines loom, danger begins. Will known landmarks rise from the sea to show your position? Are your charts accurate? I recall that during World War II our charts of New Guinea read "Reefs reported by D'Entrecasteaux, 1798." Or—even more disturbing— a reef might be noted as "Position doubtful."

Nowadays, for most of us the ocean is just an expanse of time to be flown over, so it is hard to fathom just what going to sea meant even a century ago. For one thing, it meant a hideous loss of life. In 1830 alone, for instance, Lloyd's of London reported 677 British ships lost; in 1881 there were 973.

To my knowledge, nobody has accurate figures on the number of wrecks along this "bare and bended arm of Massachusetts," as Thoreau called Cape Cod in the 1850's. But it seemed made for disaster, for a simple reason. Prevailing gales swept helpless sailing ships down on the long stretches of shifting shoals and cliffs. This was the dreaded "lee shore" of every wind sailor's nightmare. The toll in lives was immense.

For instance, in November, 1789, a storm dumped *six feet* of snow on Cape Cod and drove seven vessels ashore. Not a single crewman survived, and twenty-five bodies washed up on the beaches. The Great October Gale of 1841 caught most of the fishing fleet and destroyed it. Tiny East Dennis lost twenty men.

Small wonder, then, that Cape Cod and the islands nearby were studded with lighthouses: eighteen on Cape Cod, three on Nantucket, five on Martha's Vineyard, and two on the Elizabeth Islands.*

All followed the basic principles of the first lighthouse builder, Sostratos of Cnidos. About 300 B.C. he erected his immense tower at Alexandria in Egypt. The Cape's first light, Highland (or Cape Cod) Light, was placed on the highest ground, with the lantern 183 feet above the sea. Others followed, each set where it could best serve. This is their story—but even more it is the story of the men and women who served them.

But before the story begins I must mention and thank the many people whose help made this history possible. Wherever I turned for help I got it. And please forgive the length of this thank you list. I include (I hope) everyone who assisted materially in the research. I begin with my wife Ruth, who put up with me during the past two years. Then I must add my brother, Dr. Carl Clark of Baltimore and my college classmate Louis Dolbeare and his wife Cushing of Washington. Next I should list Arthur Railton of the Vineyard, Jacqueline Haring of Nantucket, and Janet Bosworth of Cuttyhunk, who provided much information and photographs. They also read (and corrected details of) my chapters on those islands. Anne Tait of the Massachusetts Historical Commission provided their data on lighthouses submitted for the National Register of Historic Places—invaluable material.

But beyond them is a host of people to whom I owe thanks:

♦ Mrs. B. J. Allen and Gordon Russell of the Truro Historical Society;
♦ Clair Baisly, my former student, for many photographs;
♦ Ken Black of the Seashore Museum, Rockport, Maine, for publications;
♦ The Thornton Burgess Society for photographs from Colonel Eugene Clark's collection;

---

* Readers unfamiliar with the area may wish to consult the book's end papers to locate the lighthouses as they are discussed.

◆ Gordon Caldwell and Steve Heaslip of the *Cape Cod Times* for photos;

◆ Cape Cod Photo Supply for many photographs;

◆ John Crocker of Barnstable for permission to quote Baxter logs;

◆ Tom Dorsey, my old shipmate, of Falmouth, for Naushon material;

◆ Clive Driver of the Provincetown Museum for Pamet material;

◆ Florence Fitts of the Falmouth Historical Society for keepers' logs;

◆ Alice Gibbs of the Bourne Historical Society for Wing's Neck material;

◆ David Grose of Dennis for drawings of Billingsgate's destruction;

◆ George Harding of Chatham for Stage Harbor material;

◆ Mrs. Irving Henderson of Chatham for "Chatham Twins" material;

◆ Mrs. E. Justin Hills of Harwich for her father's Monomoy diary;

◆ Parker Jones of Brewster for reproducing stacks of photographs;

◆ William E. Joseph of Eastham for Highland Light photographs;

◆ Richard Cooper Kelsey of Chatham for photographs;

◆ Susan Raidy Klein of the Kittredge Maritime Historical Research Center;

◆ Chief Gerard Lowther, USCG, for Race Point memories;

◆ the Harry Parkingtons, who live in the Mayo's Beach keeper's house;

◆ the Peak family of Hyannis for information on Point Gammon, etc.;

◆ Senior Chief Greg Peterson, USCG, for information on modern optics;

◆ Charlotte Price, Archivist, Cape Cod Community College;

◆ Bill Quinn, author and photographer, for many photographs;

◆ Walter Rogers of North Truro for help on Pamet Light;

◆ Dr. Robert Scheina, Coast Guard Historian, in Washington;

◆ Dr. Richard Sommers for current photographs from the water;

◆ Mrs. South and William Sherman of the National Archives;

◆ the Stone family, owners of the Lighthouse Inn (Bass River Light);

◆ Millard Tibbets of Orleans for memories of growing up at Highland;

◆ Peter Trull of Brewster for his "Monomoy Sunset" photograph;

◆ Martha Underwood of the Wellfleet Historical Society;

◆ the U.S. Corps of Engineers office in Buzzards Bay;

◆ Wally Welch of Opopka, Florida, for photography;

◆ Mike Whatley, Historian of the National Seashore, for "Three Sisters" material;

◆ Wayne Wheeler, U.S. Lighthouse Society, for valuable criticism;

◆ Gretchen Widegren, Cape Cod Community College, for photography;

◆ Rulon Wilcox of Great Island for photographs and a tour of the island;

◆ Barbara Williams, owner/editor of the *Barnstable Patriot*.

This has been a labor of love (to coin a phrase!), and one which I have thoroughly enjoyed. My hope is that the thousands of lighthouse *aficionadas* and *aficionados* (as well as many others) will find this story of the Cape and Island lighthouses and their people—especially the people—as engrossing as I found it to be.

Admont Gulick Clark
Dennis, Cape Cod, Massachusetts

A Brief History of Lighthouses and Their Technology

*N*obody can say when man first conceived of using shore lights to guide seagoing vessels; the answer is buried in prehistory. Some say that Homer's *Iliad* mentions such lights. Virgil in his *Aeneid* certainly does. Some also say that the Colossus at Rhodes, built about 300 B.C., showed a light in his hand. In any case, D. Alan Stevenson, the great Scotch lighthouse engineer, says that there were eighteen reputed lighthouses, from the Bosporus to Dover, before the birth of Christ.

But the most famous of the early lighthouses was the Pharos of Alexandria, in Egypt, built by Sostratos of Cnidos in about 280 B.C. This immense stone tower was 450 feet tall. For centuries it maintained a perpetual wood fire fed by slaves at its top. About 1200 A.D. an earthquake destroyed it. Edrisi, an Arab geographer, visited it in 1150, describing it thus: "During the night it shines like a star; by day you may distinguish the smoke."

And so a lighthouse became known as a *pharos*. As late as 1755 Dr. Samuel Johnson's famous dictionary defined the word as: "an high building at the top of which are hung lights to guide ships at sea."

Every pharos builder since Sostratos has followed his plan for location, height, and the best possible light. For most of history the "best possible" was a wood fire, even down to 1800. Candles came into use in the 1600's; the famous Eddystone Light used sixty large candles in an iron framework in

Figure 1.1   Cordouan tower, completed in 1611.

1697. Next came oil lamps, frequently only wicks floating in a bowl of oil—often called "spider lamps." Today two *million* candlepower is not unusual.

One of the greatest lighthouses is the French Cordouan Tower on the Bay of Biscay. Completed in 1611, it is still today one of the finest lighthouses ever built. It is a magnificent structure, 197 feet tall, highly decorated in the style of the 17th century. The base, 134 feet in diameter, contains the keepers' quarters; above are a vaulted hall 52 feet in diameter and other spaces. Today, modernized, it still shines forth.

The history of lighthouses must include Eddystone—the first one fully exposed to the fury of the sea. Today the fourth Eddystone, nine miles south of Plymouth, England, stands on a reef amid heavy traffic, hence its

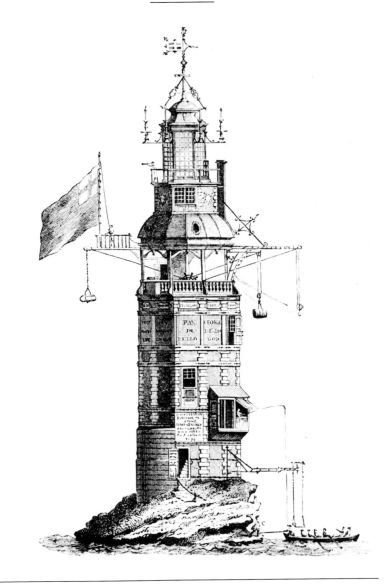

Figure 1.2   Winstanley's 1697 Eddystone tower.

importance. In 1696 Henry Winstanley spent 8000 pounds of his own money to erect a granite tower (incorporating keepers' quarters) on a rock just above high tide.

The next year, not satisfied, he built a larger, stronger tower around the first one. It lasted until the night of November 27, 1703. A terrible storm wiped out all traces of the tower, the two keepers, and Winstanley, who was there on an inspection trip.

The light soon became the subject of a sailors' chantey, so famous (or infamous) was Eddystone. Here are the words and music, still sung today:

THE EDDYSTONE LIGHT

2. One night as I was trimmin' o' the glim
   A-singin' a verse o' the evenin' hymn,
   Off to starboard there came an "Ahoy!"
   And there was me mother, a-sittin' on a buoy!

CHORUS

3. "What has become of my children three?"
   Me mother then she asked of me.
   "One was exhibited as a talkin' fish.
   The other was served in a chafin' dish!'

CHORUS

4. I looked at me mother with her seaweed hair;
   I looked again and me mother wasn't there.
   Came a voice from far away, out o' the night,
   "To Hell with the keeper of the Eddystone Light!'

Figure 1.3   Words and music, "Eddystone Light."

The *Massachusetts Gazette* on March 16, 1772, reported on an early attempt to improve the quality of the light:

> *We are informed that great Improvement hath lately been made in the Method of illuminating Lighthouses. . . . In the former Method the Oil decreasing left the Wick dry, which of course occasioned a faint Light; . . . To remedy which,* Fountain Lamps *are constructed that burn 20 Hours without any seeming Decrease of Oil, by which Means the Wick has the oil floating constantly to it and wants no Snuffing (at most but once in a Night). . . .*

But it was a Frenchman, Ami Argand, who in 1792 developed the first major advance in lighting. It was a nearly smokeless lamp with a glass chimney and a reservoir for oil. The remaining problem was to direct the most light to the horizon. Eventually a parabolic reflector, coated with silver, proved to be the most efficient. And so numerous Argand lamps, each with its own reflector, were mounted in large iron frames.

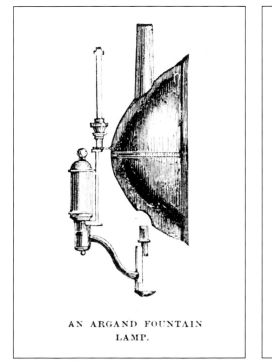

AN ARGAND FOUNTAIN
LAMP.

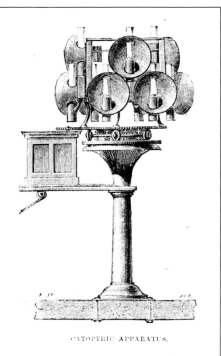

CATOPTRIC APPARATUS.

Figure 1.4 Argand's fountain lamp with reflector.

Figure 1.5 Revolving mechanism with Argand lamps.

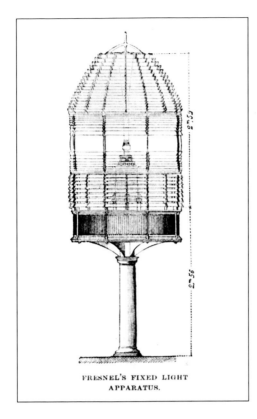

FRESNEL'S FIXED LIGHT
APPARATUS.

Figure 1.6   Fresnel fixed light apparatus.

Later the *Nantucket Weekly Mirror* reported in 1856 on experiments to determine the efficiency of various systems:

> *We find by experiment, that with an open light, twenty-nine thirtieths [97 percent] of the whole light is lost. . . . By means of the best modeled reflectors, five thirtieths [17 percent] . . . is saved and rendered useful. By means of the dioptric apparatus [the Fresnel lens] five sixths [83 percent] of the light is rendered available.*

This ultimate in light control was the work of another Frenchman. After four years' work Augustin Fresnel developed the lens system that still bears his name. On July 25, 1823, the first revolving dioptric lens and light shone forth from the great Cordouan Lighthouse. These early lenses were built up of curved prisms of glass mounted in a metal frame. There were different sizes, depending on the importance of the light. The smallest was a little gem of a lens only 11-3/4 inches in diameter. The largest was a huge crystal like the one installed in Highland (Cape Cod) Light in 1901. It stood twelve feet high, with a diameter of nine feet, weighed 2000 pounds, and floated in a circular bed of mercury. And one oil lamp, with a 4-inch-diameter wick, could reach the horizon, twenty-five miles away.

Such a lens crystal conveys a feeling of sheer power and skill. Perhaps D. Alan Stevenson, a cousin of Robert Louis Stevenson and a great lighthouse engineer, describes it best:

> *Nothing can be more beautiful than an entire apparatus of a fixed light of the first order. It consists of a central belt of refractors . . . ; [above and below] it are six triangular rings of glass, forming by their union a hollow cage, I know of no work of art more beautiful or creditable to the boldness, ardor, intelligence, and zeal of the artist.*

While whale oil was the primary fuel in early days, the Lighthouse Service had long been interested in mineral oils. As early as 1807 Albert Gallatin, Secretary of the Treasury, had corresponded with the owners of the *Coromandel*, from Rangoon, Burma. She had a cargo of 5000 gallons of "earth oil," claimed by her owners to be

> *the very best article for burning in lighthouses, making a very strong, clear, and bright flame, emitting at the same time a great volume of smoak.*

Needless to say, the service did not buy the cargo, because of the "smoak."

Lamps need oil. Lighthouse Service records tell of a continuing quest for a cheaper, better fuel—especially when whale oil rose in price from ninety cents a gallon to $2.43. They even tried colza oil, squeezed from the seeds of the wild cabbage and widely used in France. In fact, they tried to establish colza as a new farm crop in this country, but failed. Lard oil was used for quite a while, too, and experiments tried out shark, fish, olive, and mineral oils. Finally, as the petroleum industry developed, they turned to kerosene (or "coal oil" as it was first called).

Gradually the problems of storing a volatile, flammable fuel were solved. Kerosene gave one-fifth more light and cost much less: in 1882 lard oil cost fifty-seven cents a gallon; kerosene cost eight cents. Even gas had its day; for example, until the mid-1960's acetylene gas was the major fuel for lighted buoys. And all over the country solid brick or metal oil houses were built to safely store the kerosene. By 1890 almost all light stations had oil houses, despite problems of getting Congress to fund construction of these inexpensive—yet most necessary—structures. Many of them still exist today.

Finally came electricity, first at the Hell Gate Tower in New York's East River. The effect was grand, but the nine 6000-candlepower lamps dazzled the ships' pilots. And so in 1886 the 225-foot tower was razed. But soon electricity became standard for lighthouses. A frequent source today is one 1000-watt lamp, producing a million or more candlepower through the lens system.

But however good a lighthouse, its lamps, its fuel, its keeper's dedication, FOG can totally obscure a light, even when radar lets us "see" through it. It seems strange that lighthouse engineers took so long to find a solution. A fog bell in a Norwegian lighthouse in 1766 was a distinct novelty. Boston Light had a "great Gun to answer ships in Fogg." But it was seldom used.

The problem was a lack of technology and better materials. In 1811 Bell Rock in the North Sea had a large bell struck every thirty seconds by a clockworks. Finally steam came to the rescue, with large steam-generated fog signals like the Daboll fog trumpet. Cumbersome and inefficient, it produced a characteristic deep, far-reaching moan.

Early in this century Isaac Small described the trumpet at Highland (Cape Cod) Light:

> *It was run during thick weather and operated by air pressure. The three engines in their 12-foot by 24-foot house were caloric and the heat generated [created air pressure], forcing the air out through the trumpet [causing] a hoarse blast which . . . could be heard for miles.*

Today's fog signals are little different, but operated electrically.

Lighthouse history in North America begins a mere twenty years after Eddystone. In 1713 a committee of merchants and shipmasters in Boston proposed "the Erecting of a Light House and Lanthorn." Two years later the General Court (the legislature) approved, noting that lack of a light "hath been a great discouragement to navigation by the loss of the Lives and Estates of Several of His Majesties Subjects." And so, on September 17, 1716, Boston Light on Little Brewster Island was lit.

The first keeper was Captain George Worthylake, a retired mariner. He and his wife and daughter drowned in 1718 while returning to the lighthouse after collecting his pay in Boston—"fifty pounds . . . for the Hire of a person to take care of the Light House for the first Year."

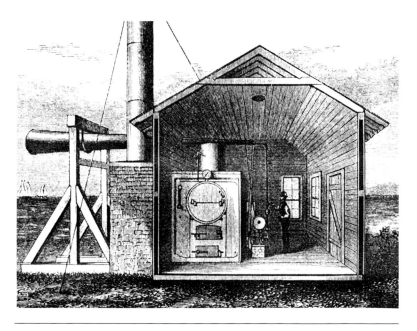

Figure 1.7   Steam fog-horn (sectional view).

Recently a long-lost sermon of Puritan divine Cotton Mather came to light in Salem, Massachusetts. On November 9, 1718, he presided at the funeral of the three Worthylakes and others. Two other Worthylake children on the island saw the disaster and could do nothing. He said:

> *Tho they were now so near the shoar, yet the winds and the seas, were so high they could not fetch it, before they were all of them unhappily drowned. . . . Imagine if thou canst, the agony. The dead bodies of their parents and sister and others being throun upon the land, were the only company which these poor children had upon the desolate island for two whole days and nights together.*

Boston Light burned several times, was blown up by the British in 1776, and was rebuilt in 1783. It still stands, though often struck by lightning. In 1788 lightning rods were installed. This was done although the prevailing belief was that "for the arm of the flesh to avert the stroke of heaven" was irreligious. In 1789 Congress declared all twelve colonial lighthouses United States property. All are still in operation.

And Cape Cod still offered its fanged shore to any passing ship. By 1802 the Humane Society of Boston, a voluntary life-saving group, had built six

Figure 1.8   Boston Light, built in 1716.

"houses of refuge" (and more later) along the Atlantic coast of Cape Cod. Stranded seamen (and there were hundreds of them) could at least shelter from the weather in them. Dr. James Freeman of Wellfleet described these huts in 1802 as being "eight feet long, eight feet wide, and seven feet high. . . , supplied with either straw or hay . . . and farther accommodated with a bench."

They served until 1872, when nine stations of the Life-Saving Service were built and manned between Provincetown and Monomoy. Today the Coast Guard has the duty of saving lives and property, as well as tending the lights, all but one of which (Boston) are automated.

In the earliest United States lighthouses spider lamps (open containers of oil with wicks, little better than candles) were in use until about 1810. Then the Lewis imitations of Argand lamps with parabolic reflectors were adopted until about 1850, when widespread use of the Fresnel lenses finally appeared.

Within the last decade all of the active lighthouses under consideration here (except Great Point on Nantucket, which is a replica built after the great storm of 1984) and the inactive Monomoy Light have been put on the National Register of Historic Places.

A Brief History
of the Lighthouse
Establishment

*A*t least a century before the signing of the Constitution the various colonies had felt the need for aid to their growing maritime interests. The first publicly financed light is revealed in a petition from the citizens of Nantasket (now Hull), Massachusetts, to the General Court. They asked for relief from taxes because they had built and supplied a beacon on Point Allerton (just south of Boston harbor) with "fier bales of pitch and ocum." These were burned at the top of a tower.

But the first true lighthouse was Boston's, built in 1716 at a cost of 2,285 pounds. All inbound and outbound vessels except coasters paid light dues of one penny per ton; the dues paid for upkeep of the lighthouse.

The other colonies followed suit, until by 1789 lighthouses also existed at Nantucket; Tybee Island, Georgia; Narragansett Bay; New London, Connecticut; Sandy Hook, New York; Cape Henlopen; Charleston, South Carolina; Portsmouth, New Hampshire; and Plymouth, Cape Ann, and Naushon Island in Massachusetts.

One of the first acts of the First Congress (its ninth, in fact) provided for transfer of colonial lighthouses to the new government:

That all expenses which shall accrue from and after the 15th day of August, 1789, in the necessary support, maintenance, and repairs

**Figure 2.1   Stephen Pleasonton,
Fifth Auditor of the Treasury.
Courtesy of U.S. Lighthouse Society.**

*of all lighthouses, beacons, buoys and public piers, placed or sunk
before the passage of this Act . . . shall be defrayed out of the treasury
of the United States.*

Alexander Hamilton, first Secretary of the Treasury, became responsible
for all aids to navigation, with local control by the collectors of customs in
each port. Collectors were political appointees of the party in power, and so
even the keepers of lights tended to be "party men" for the most part. But the
loyalty and attention to duty of most keepers (often under primitive living
conditions) is legendary.

Until 1820 the Lighthouse Service seemed an orphan, serving under four
different agencies in those thirty-one years. Finally, it was reassigned to
Treasury, under control of the Fifth Auditor, Stephen Pleasonton. He was a
fine, cautious accountant, but he knew nothing about lighthouses. Even so, in
the years until 1852 he presided over an increase from 55 aids to navigation
of all sorts to 325.

Pleasonton solved his problems of construction and supply by contract-
ing out the work to the lowest bidder. This bidder was a Cape Codder,

Captain Winslow Lewis of Wellfleet (1770–1850). In 1808 he had invented a "reflecting and magnifying lantern," which was a copy of the Argand lamp. The government bought his patent for $20,000.

Winslow Lewis had bid on the contract "for fitting up and keeping in repair, any or all of the light-houses in the United States or territories thereof" for seven years. He had to guarantee that the lights would be brighter and would use half as much oil. In fact he was so successful that in 1816 his contract was renewed, and since his lamps reduced oil consumption by 70 percent he did well. That year he made a net profit of $12,472.38—almost half of the President's salary then. So began a career during which he built many lighthouses and refitted over ninety.

When he died in 1850 (at eighty) he received an unusual tribute—an editorial obituary in the *Boston Journal*:

> *The services which he has rendered the government and our mercantile interests . . . have been incalculable, and will cause his name to be long held in respect and veneration by all who have business on the great ocean.*

But all was not well with the service. As it grew, Pleasonton found himself less and less able to cope with the multiplicity of details. Harsh criticism came from many quarters. The publishers of *Blunt's Coast Pilot* and many shipmasters pointed out the poor quality and confusing displays of our lighthouses compared to Europe's. Ours were almost all fixed white lights; Europe's had revolving and different-colored lights as well as the powerful Fresnel lenses.

Responding to the criticism, in 1837–1838 Congress moved to make some changes. First, the Board of Naval Commissioners must approve all lighthouse appropriations. Second, the Senate voted to import and test two large Fresnel lenses (They cost too much, said Pleasonton). The test, at Navesink, showed that the lenses were far superior to our lamps and reflectors—and much less expensive to operate. Only one lamp in a Fresnel lens outshone twenty-four of the old style and used a fraction of the oil.

To illustrate how antiquated our system was, in 1838 Lewis built three fixed lighthouses at Nauset on Cape Cod, to avoid confusion with the nearby Chatham twin lights. Yet since 1823 revolving light technology and the new lenses had been widely used in Europe. At Nauset three lamps in Fresnel lenses could have replaced the *thirty* lamps in the three towers. That same

Figure 2.2 Walter Forward, Secretary of the Treasury. Courtesy of U.S. Lighthouse Society.

year Lieutenant Edward Carpender, USN, made this suggestion; it was not followed.

In 1842 a Committee on Commerce study generally glossed over the problem with the statement: "When an old and well-tried system works tolerably well, change and experiment should be avoided." However, Secretary of the Treasury Walter Forward hired Isaiah William Penn Lewis, a respected engineer and nephew of Winslow Lewis, to survey all of the New England lighthouses.

His report was another indictment. For example, "From Monhegan Island [in Maine] seven fixed lights are visible [from one location]." Pity the poor sailor trying to figure out where he was!

Lewis's report was almost totally damning. Sarcastically he called the two Nantucket Cliff range lights "a very excellent invention for manufacturing lampblack at the expense of one hundred and fifty gallons of oil per annum." Of the keeper's quarters he said:

> *Those who had a decent roof to cover their heads appeared industrious and happy . . . and their lanterns in perfect order; while those*

whose homes were in a state of partial ruin ... and who are compelled to seek their daily supply of fresh water among the hollows and clefts of the rocks had a look of squalid wretchedness about them, their houses and lanterns were filthy and unclean, and their families ragged and dirty.

Naturally Pleasonton defended his administration, declaring himself "grossly misrepresented." He sent his boss, the Treasury Secretary, the names of 1,000 captains attesting to the excellence of the system. This act postponed for eight years his "dethroning."

In 1845 two Navy officers went to Europe to study ways by which our system could be improved. Their detailed 1846 report recommended sweeping changes, most of which Congress adopted in 1851. At the same time Congress ordered placement of Fresnel lenses in lighthouses "as rapidly as [the Secretary of the Treasury] thought best."

Complying with the legislation, Secretary Corwin named a board of Navy, Army, and Coast Survey officers as an *ad hoc* committee to recommend a new system. Promptly they produced a huge (760-page) report setting forth in detail how the service should be run. This committee became the Lighthouse Board, which would be in charge of the Lighthouse Service for the next fifty-eight years.

The new board took immediate steps to improve the situation. By 1859 nearly all of the old reflector systems had been replaced by Fresnel lenses. The board went on to develop more effective fog signals, the bell buoy, a uniform system of buoyage ("Red Right Returning," as every sailor knows), and the critically important *Notices to Mariners*.

The Civil War devastated the service. Some 174 lighthouses went out of commission, many lightships were sunk, and officers were involved in war duties. But shortly after the war things were back nearly to normal. In 1874 Congress added the Mississippi and tributaries to the board's duties and later added the outlying possessions.

With the new century many changes occurred. In 1903 Congress created the Commerce Department and transferred jurisdiction over the Lighthouse Board to that agency. Then in 1910 the board was abolished, and the new civilian-operated Bureau of Lighthouses was created. In its fifty-eight years the Lighthouse Board increased lighted aids from 335 to almost 4,000 and buoys from 1,000 to 5,300 and made great strides in technological innovation. Each of the eighteen new districts was run by a civilian District Inspector (later Superintendent), all directly under a Commissioner of Lighthouses.

Figure 2.3   Admiral William Shubrick, first head of the Lighthouse Board (1852–1871). Courtesy of U.S. Lighthouse Society.

Figure 2.4   George Putnam, first Commissioner of Lighthouses (1910–1935). Courtesy of his daughter, Mrs. John Hay.

The first commissioner was George Putnam, already a veteran of the Coast and Geodetic Survey. His twenty-five year tenure saw a doubling of aids, while personnel dropped from 5,832 to 4,980. His successor was H.D. King, who served until July 1, 1939, when President Roosevelt consolidated the Coast Guard and the Lighthouse Service under the Treasury Department.

Under the presidential order, keepers could either resign, retire (with enough time), stay as civilian members of the USCG, or transfer to the Coast Guard with no loss of pay. A great many chose the transfer option since as civilians they were draft-eligible, and World War II was looming on the horizon.

The 1950's and 1960's saw a gradual transition to Coast Guard manning of the lighthouses. The last civilian keeper was Frank Schubert at Coney Island, and by the mid-1980's most lights were fully automated. Today only Boston Light remains as a manned lighthouse.

So the great era of manned lighthouses has passed. Modern electronics have replaced the devoted "keepers of the flame" of earlier times—and something precious has been lost. A slower, far more arduous, disciplined way of life is no more. *Perhaps* this is progress.

3

Cape Cod—The Mariner's Nightmare

Cape Cod seems built for lighthouses. This statement, absurd as it may sound, is dreadfully close to the truth. Long ago it put to sea and has been under way ever since, say old Cape Codders. They also say that "she rolls over on herself"—wrecks buried in sand on one side of the Cape turn up a hundred years later on the other side—or so they claim.

As a result, after urging by marine interests, one of the earliest acts of Congress was to start marking the path of this wandering peninsula. They authorized establishment in 1797 of the great Highland (or Cape Cod) Light; in the next hundred years they added seventeen more lights along the Cape.

There are two main reasons for this number—economy and geography. First let's take a look at the Cape Cod of 1800, dredged up aeons before by the glaciers rolling over North America. Its few inhabitants lived by the sea. They fertilized their thin, sandy soil with fish (as did the Indians), whaled and fished in the rich waters, roamed the world in their ships—and stripped the land of trees to build the ships to earn a living.

By 1800 the 10 settlers of 1639 had become 19,329 souls, gathered in little villages along the shore. Roads were ruts through the thin grass cover. A trip from Barnstable to Boston was a bone-bruising ordeal by wagon. In 1798 Provincetown's town meeting petitioned the government "for a post to come down the Cape." The response was a man on horseback, making a mail trip once a week at best.

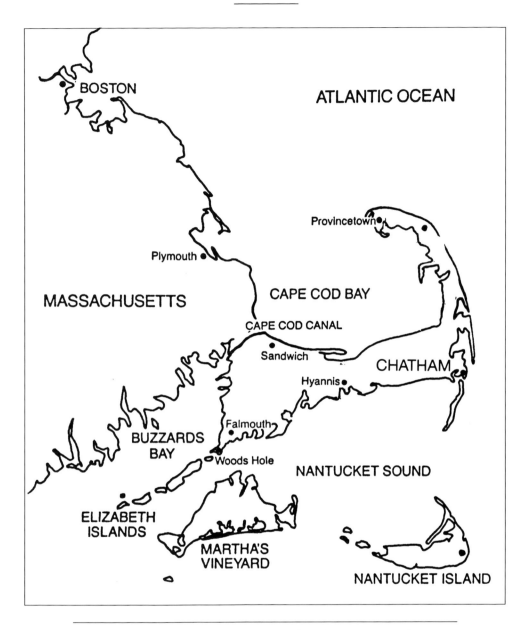

Figure 3.1   Cape Cod and the Islands. Courtesy of U.S. Lighthouse Society.

Since land travel was so difficult, Cape Codders went by sea. Almost every town developed a fast packet service to Boston, often making three trips a week. For $1.50 the packet would deliver you to Boston in six hours. Even medical emergencies went by sea. A whaleman accidentally harpooned off P'town was rushed to Boston by whaleboat carrying a double crew—the fastest ambulance service they had.

But the sea was not only a highway; it became a profitable investment. With huge tracts of sand and unlimited salt water, Cape Codders developed a new industry—salt-making. In 1776 Captain John Sears of Dennis ("Crazy John," some people called him) built the first successful salt works,

> *a vat a hundred feet long and ten feet wide. Rafters were fixed over it; and shutters were contrived to move up and down, that the vat might be covered when it rained, and exposed to the heat of the sun in fair weather,*

wrote Dr. James Freeman of Wellfleet in 1802. Captain Sears patented his idea in 1799, and improvements soon followed.

By that time nearly every enterprising native with the capital was building salt works. As early as 1802 there were already 136 works covering 1,250,000 square feet—*twenty-eight acres* of vats producing salts worth $41,700 a year. And Dr. Freeman noted that another five acres were planned for 1803.

Of course, huge quantities of this marine salt were needed to preserve the harvests of fish. For example, the typical small fisherman used about 700 barrels a year. Even so, ships were kept busy ferrying salt to Boston, New York, Philadelphia, Europe, and the West Indies. Hundreds of men prospered on sea salt alone, especially when in good times annual profits were 25 percent.

The sea was their livelihood, yes, but it took their lives with grim regularity. No gentle slave was the Atlantic. In 1815 a hurricane (Cape Codders called it a tempest) pushed the water in Buzzards Bay so high that the Cape almost became an island. In 1825 three great storms destroyed the fishing fleets, and the Great October Gale of 1841 spread death all down the Cape. Little Truro alone lost seven vessels and fifty-seven men.

The final, compelling reason for so many lights was geographic: the threat of the Cape to every passing ship. To illustrate, in 1903 the U.S. Corps of Engineers compiled a map recording the known wrecks on Cape Cod— just over 1000 of them. These sands hold—and sometimes uncover—the bones of thousands of brave men and their ships. In September, 1985, for example, Barry Clifford began to bring up the treasure from Black Bellamy's pirate ship *Whidah*, wrecked off Nauset Beach in the early 18th century.

Prevailing winds and storms make the Cape a "lee shore" of hideous length. There is no more helpless feeling than finding yourself driven by wind and wave down upon the land. The ship strikes; the masts fall with a groan; and if you are lucky she holds together long enough to drive ashore, so that you get to the beach alive—if you are lucky.

Slim indeed were your chances before 1872, when the Life-Saving Service was organized. Of course, if your body was found, the people of the town would give you a decent burial. They would even provide a monument describing your demise.

So there were plenty of reasons for lighthouses, especially along the outer Cape, facing the Atlantic Ocean. And build them we did, starting with the Highland (Cape Cod) Light in 1797. This is their history.

Highland
(Cape Cod) Light

Light List No. 475
42° 2.4' N, 70° 3.7' W
Ht. above water: 183 feet
15 lamps; 1st order Fresnel (1857, 1901); aerobeacons
Built 1797; rebuilt 1857
Range: 23 miles
Flashing white every 5 seconds
Radio beacon: 286 kHz—HI
White tower, covered way to dwelling

A deed dated August 6, 1796, in the National Archives marks the formal start of Cape Cod's lighthouse history:

Know all men by these present that I Isaac Small of Truro in the County of Barnstable traided in consideration of one hundred and ten dollars to me paid by the United States of America sile and convey unto the said states a certain piece of clean land in said Truro near a place called Clay Pounds and is bounded by the sea at high water mark [containing] pircesely ten acres . . . and also sile and convey the priviledg of passing and repassing through my land . . . said passage to be convenient for teams hors or foot with convenient gates or barrs.

The deed was recorded in the forty-ninth book of county records. But on the night of October 27, 1827, the brick—and supposedly fireproof—County House burned to the ground, destroying all the records since 1639. So this copy is a priceless bit of Cape Cod history.

The events leading up to the deed are worth telling, since they show the workings of the political process, even this early. In 1794 the Reverend Levi Whitman wrote to his good friend Dr James Freeman, suggesting a site for a lighthouse: "Why then should not that dark chasm between Cape Ann and Nantucket be illuminated?" he asked.

Dr. Freeman promptly enlisted the support of powerful merchant and shipping interests in Boston, such as the Boston Marine Society, founded in 1742. On February 2, 1796, this group adopted the following "Memorial," to be sent to Congress in Philadelphia:

> *The Boston Marine Society beg leave to represent. That the frequent shipwrecks on Cape Cod . . . renders every attempt to prevent such melancholy accidents interesting & important. The erection of a lighthouse on the Highlands of the Cape is perhaps the only measure that could aid the Navigator in this respect, upon that dangerous winter coast.*

On Isaac Small's ten acres on North Truro's Highland (pronounced as two words) the Cape Cod Light Station rose quickly. In 1797 the light was lit; President Washington named one keeper, paid $300 a year.

Some sources say that Highland was the first in this country to have a "revolving eclipser" (a shield in front of the lamps moved by clockworks). But in 1817 Winslow Lewis, who held the contract for lighthouse maintenance, published a "Description of the Light Houses," a sort of early *Notice to Mariners.* He says that "Boston contains a *revolving* light which may be seen at 9 or 10 leagues distant." About Cape Cod Light he says: "The lantern is elevated 180 feet above the sea and contains a *fixed* light, with sixteen lamps and reflectors." [Italics mine] The weight of evidence is against Captain Lewis.

A little later Henry David Thoreau stopped four times at the lighthouse during the trips he recorded in *Cape Cod.* He says:

> *Over this bare Highland the wind has full sweep. Even in July it blows the wings over the heads of young turkeys, which do not know enough to head against it; . . . and you must hold onto the lighthouse to prevent being blown into the Atlantic.*

Figure 4.1   First Highland Light.

Being a good practical surveyor, he decided to measure the angle and height of the blue clay cliff in front of the lighthouse. Lack of equipment did not stop him:

> *I borrowed the plan and square, levels and dividers of a carpenter . . . and, using one of those shingles made of a mast, contrived a rude sort of quadrant . . . and got the elevation of the bank . . . The mixed sand and clay lay at an angle of 40° with the horizon . . . , but the clay is much steeper. No cow or hen ever gets down it.*

He found that the cliff was 123 feet above the water. Today, when one stands at the top, it seems much higher than that.

Thoreau's host was keeper James Small. Along with his other duties, he was expected to count the number (and kind) of ships passing the light. In one ten-day period in 1853, Thoreau reports, 1200 ships passed.

Because of its location astride the shipping lanes, Cape Cod Light became a maritime nerve center. A later Isaac Small was stationed there as Marine Reporting Agent. His job was to telegraph to Boston news of ships headed for port, so that their owners could be ready for their arrival. Later the Navy's first radio station, NAE, was located there, and that is where the first experiments with the radio direction finder were conducted.

After sixty years at Highland, in 1928 Isaac Small wrote *Shipwrecks on Cape Cod*. He recalls vividly the first stranding he witnessed. As a boy he stood with his mother on the edge of the cliff on a foggy April afternoon in 1852 as the British bark *Josephus* broke up in the surf.

The seas were running so high that nobody could board the hulk. But Daniel Cassidy and Jonathan Collins of North Truro tried anyway, using a twelve-foot dory. Their fate:

> *I saw the little boat, with the two men pulling bravely at the oars. They had hardly gone fifty yards from the shore when a great white cataract of foam and rushing water hurled at them. The next instant it buried men and boat . . . ; two human heads rose for an instant through the seething sea . . . , and they were seen no more.*

**Figure 4.2   Second Highland Light. Rosenthal photo,
courtesy of Cape Cod Photo Supply.**

With darkness the people on shore gave up hope of saving any of the crew, but the keeper refused to quit. By keeping a vigil, he found two men alive who had finally washed ashore.

Five years later, in 1857, the first tower was declared unsafe and a new tower replaced it. And the government's original ten acres at the top of the 123-foot cliff are now about two—thanks to erosion. In fact, the fog signal has had to be moved back several times since 1872.

Improvements to this crucial light continued. Into the new tower went an entirely new lens and lamp system costing $30,000. The single oil lamp had four concentric wicks, and the lens was the largest available from France—nearly twelve feet high and six feet in diameter—a huge diamond of a Fresnel lens.

Now that Cape Cod was a first-order light, it needed more keepers. Horace Hughes received $500 a year, and his two assistants, James Small and Thomas Kenney, received $300. A few of their duties included lighting the lamp exactly at sunset; standing four-hour watches until sunrise; trimming the wicks (keepers were often called "Wickies"); seeing that the oil pump to the lamp kept going; and operating the Daboll fog signal when needed. This last duty combined the jobs of fireman and mechanic (as necessary). They had to stoke the coal fire of the "caloric engine," producing the air pressure to make the gargantuan moan of the trumpet.

During the last half of the century a rising tide of criticism of the light came from pilots and shipmasters. For many, the light was not distinctive enough; they said they often mistook it for a ship's masthead light. At last, in 1899, the Boston Chamber of Commerce persuaded the Lighthouse Board to act.

A huge new revolving lens was ordered from France, and in October, 1901, the room-sized crystal went into position, floating on a circular bed of mercury. The clockworks turned the lens so that there was a half-second flash and a four-and-a-half-second interval (as it is today) with the same four-wick lamp. In 1932 a 1000-watt electric lamp went in. It produced a beam so powerful that its loom against clouds has been seen forty-five miles away.

But what about the human side of these light stations—the boredom of endless hours of watch, the thousand and one jobs involved in the light and the station, the family life?

Millard Tibbetts of Orleans recalled vividly his boyhood days at Cape Cod Light. His father, Fred W. Tibbetts, came to Highland in 1912 from Spectacle Island and spent twenty-six years as assistant and head keeper at Highland. 1912 was the year that the keepers' houses received central heat. And each had a coal ration of seven tons, no matter how cold the winters were.

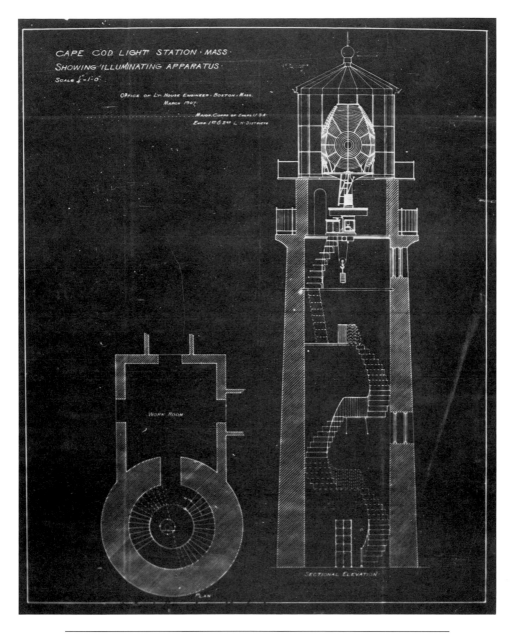

**Figure 4.3   Engineering drawing of light, 1907. U.S. Coast
Guard photo.**

**Figure 4.4　View inside first-order lens. Courtesy of William
E. Joseph.**

It was a fine place for a boy to grow up. During summers the nearby
Highland House (run by Hayes Small) was full of guests; the three keepers had
their families; the radio station personnel were there; Isaac Small had his family
there; and Ed Larkin had a whole passel of sons and daughters down the road.

In short, the lighthouse was the center of a whole community. The
children walked the two miles to North Truro center to school, and the big
event of the day was to see the train come through of an evening.

But while a boy could make his own fun, living at the light was sheer
drudgery for the keepers' wives, as for women everywhere then. There was
no running water, and inside toilets were still in the future. The black iron

Figure 4.5   Keeper William A. Joseph (1923–1947). Courtesy of William E. Joseph.

stove and the soapstone sink were the two poles of a woman's existence. And when a keeper fell ill his wife naturally took over his watch and other duties—and sometimes became keeper when he died.

Existence required much more effort then. A round trip to Truro, eight miles away, took all day. But even the children absorbed something of the meaning of the great crystal light their fathers served. It stood for something strong and benevolent, a symbol of the power whose shores it guarded. In his seven years at Highland Light Station, young Millard certainly absorbed it, before going to sea in 1919.

The great classic first-order lens served well for over fifty years. Finally, in the early 1950's, it was dismantled and replaced by a pair of Fresnel-lensed aerobeacons mounted vertically and at right angles. Inside each beacon are two 1000-watt lamps (the spare flips into place if the first one fails) and an additional pair of concentrating lenses. Today the light is fully automated and monitored from the Chatham Coast Guard Station. Coast Guard families occupy the quarters.

But like Sankaty Head on Nantucket, Block Island Southeast, and others before them, the Cape Cod Lighthouse is in danger from further erosion.

Figure 4.6   Recent airview of Highland Light. Photo by Richard Cooper Kelsey.

Gordon Russell, president of the Truro Historical Society, noted that a 117-foot section of the cliff disappeared during the winter of 1990. There is little room left in front of the lighthouse. His society is mounting a drive to move the tower back from the edge of the cliff, a move that would probably cost several million dollars. And so a newly formed town committee is seeking federal, state and foundation funding. The lighthouse would probably be located on nearby National Seashore land—rather than be lost to the sea.

5

Chatham Light ("The Chatham Twins")

Light List No. 505
41° 40.3' N, 69° 57' W
Ht. above water: 80 feet
6 lamps per tower; 4th-order Fresnels (1857);
*   aerobeacons (1969)*
Built 1808; rebuilt 1841, 1881
Range: 28 miles
Flashing white 2 ev. 10 seconds
Radio beacon: 311 kHz—CH
Storm warnings by day
White conical tower

*C*ape Cod's second lighthouse, like many others, has struggled with encroaching seas. Twice since 1808 the Atlantic has swallowed the towers and portions of the cliff on which they stand. The present lighthouse has survived (so far) for over a hundred years.

After Cape Cod Light, the next logical spot for a lighthouse was on James's Bluff in the center of Chatham. Two lights there (to distinguish them from Highland Light) would help ships make the dangerous passage from Nantucket Sound up along the Cape, with its shifting reefs and shoals. The winning contractor had planned to use local rock for the towers, but he could find none.

Figure 5.1   First "Chatham Twins." Courtesy of Mrs. Irving Henderson.

Clearly he was unfamiliar with the local geology: the southern half of Cape Cod is mostly one long sandpile. In June, 1806, he reported plaintively: "There are no stones so the towers will have to be made of wood."

Then someone suggested that wooden towers could be made movable to act as *range lights** for the shifting harbor entrance. Accordingly, on June 18, 1807, the *Columbian Centinel* published revised specifications. The towers "shall be of wood and the form octagon," to be set on wooden skids to form a range. They were to be:

> *of good oak or white pine without sap, and to be 22 feet in diameter at the commencement. The height of the pyramid to be 40 feet from the stonework foundation to the floor of the lantern [the glassed-in room where the light is] where the diameter is to be 8 feet.*

Specifications also called for building a keeper's house, seventeen by twenty-six feet, with a parlor, bedroom, kitchen, and cellar. Two fireplaces for heat

*Range lights are pairs of lights in line to mark a safe channel. If the lights line up, the ship is in the channel. If not, it may be in danger.

were included. And so the towers were built. Each tower had six oil lamps, backed by 8½-inch reflectors and mounted on a circular iron frame.

On October 7, 1808, President Jefferson appointed Samuel Nye the first keeper, pleasing some 150 Chatham citizens who had signed a petition in his behalf. Then came Joseph Loveland, followed by Samuel Stinson. Apparently Stinson did not take his duties too seriously. Several times during 1832 he neglected the lights and was warned by the district superintendent. Soon after the last warning he resigned, asking to be paid for an addition to the house. But his request was denied because he had not received authorization to do it.

Winslow Lewis's "Description of the Light-Houses" says:

Chatham having a barred harbor, and frequently shifting, two lights were erected for the purpose of moving as the bar changed, so as to keep both lights in one, as a leading mark over the bar, but this has proved impracticable, owing to the very great and sudden changes of the bar. —The lanterns . . . are very useful to vessels bound over Nantucket Shoals.

These original towers lasted until 1841. As the result of an inspection by Lieutenant Edward Carpender, USN, in 1838, they were abandoned as:

very much shaken and decayed, so as to make it dangerous to ascend them in windy weather. They each contain 6 lamps, with 8½ inch reflectors, and with plano-convex lenses of green glass, 9 inches [in diameter] in front of them.

These lenses were part of Winslow Lewis's patented invention that actually reduced the light from his lamps, basically copies of Argand's original design. And Lewis's reflectors were, as someone said, "as parabolic as a barber's wash basin." They were covered with a thin coat of silver that quickly wore off under the polishing by ill-trained keepers.

In 1841 new forty-foot brick towers were built farther back from the edge of the bluff. Each received nine lamps with fourteen-inch reflectors. Collins Howes, who had lost a leg in a fishing accident, became the first keeper of the new lights. He lasted until 1845, when a change of administrations in Washington ousted him. But he did not give up without a fight. His successor, Simeon Nickerson, died in 1848, and Simeon's destitute widow, Angeline, became keeper. Howes began a letter campaign against her.

This irked Joshua Nickerson of Chatham, whose ancestors had bought

Chatham's land from the Indians. He wrote the President a strong letter on April 19, 1849:

> *The appointment of [Simeon's] widow, so far as I know, gave general satisfaction. —of one thing, I am certain which is, that she had discharged her duties . . . in a most careful and faithful manner.*

Mrs. Nickerson remained keeper for many years.

Charles Smith was the next keeper when in 1857 the old reflectors and lamps went out and fixed fourth-order Fresnel lenses and single lamps were installed. They lasted until 1923.

But the Atlantic was not yet through with the Chatham Twins. Captain Josiah Hardy became keeper on December 6, 1872, and carefully recorded the inroads of the seas on the cliff. On November 15, 1870, a powerful storm had broken through the outer barrier beaches (it happened again in 1988) and destroyed piers in the harbor. The lights were then 228 feet from the edge of the bluff.

Figure 5.2 Ruins of the second "Twins." Courtesy of Mrs. Irving Henderson.

**Figure 5.3   Third Chatham Lights. Courtesy of Mrs. Irving
Henderson.**

Captain Hardy's log reports on December 21, 1874: "The distance was
measured today, from foot of south tower to edge of bank was 190 feet." In
four years thirty-eight feet of a forty-foot high bluff had toppled into the sea.
Erosion increased. In 1876 the log records a mere ninety-five feet, half the
1874 distance. Finally, on December 15, 1879, at 1:00 P.M. the south tower slid
over the bank. And in fifteen months the other tower and the keeper's house
went. So in nine years the sea had carved from the bluff three-quarters of a
football field.

Another set of Twins, of the latest design (curved iron plates bolted
together and lined with brick) arose even farther back, together with a double
keepers' house. A fine design it was, with many others around the country
still functioning. Keeper Hardy moved his family into the new house. The
lamps still used lard oil, but in July 1882, they were converted to "coal oil"
(kerosene).

Josiah Hardy retired after twenty-eight years of service, leaving behind
his logs as a priceless record of his times. For example, he tells of the coming
of the railroad to Chatham:

Wednesday, May 18, 1887 The first shovelful of sand was broken and thrown out on the commencement of the Chatham to Harwich Rail Road.

October 18, 1887 the laying of the streight Rails . . . was completed So that the Engine come to Chatham depot @ 12 M in commemoration of the Event Church and School bells were rung & steam Whistle blown in great dexterity.

November 19, 1887 P.M. the first Passenger train come down from the Old colony [Railroad] with ten Passengers. . . . A free ride is given all Day to & from Harwich . . .

Hardy was no hermit. He also kept abreast of local and national events in the backs of his annual logs:

June 29, 1875—Mrs. Albert Smith committed suicide at 4 am with a knife in her own house.

Sept. 19, 1881—@ 10:35 pm James A Garfield, President of the U.S. departed this life from wound received from the hands of Guiteau on July 3, 1881. . . .

Friday—30 June [1882] SW to South cloudy unsettled weather Guiteau Charles J. Guiteau, the Presidential assassin was hung today in Washington, D.C. for shooting President Garfield.

Wednesday—July 5 [1882] NE fresh gales and Rain all day Latter part fog the sea nocked the old Lumber Schooner all to pieces. She was sold to David Gould for $7.00

Reading these pages is a real pleasure because they reveal so much about life in his time. He recorded the death of Vice President Hammond "of Parralysis of the heart" on the day it happened. What a contrast to the dreary acres of lighthouse logs recording nothing but "SSW gales. Rain." His final terse entry on June 28, 1897, was: "WSW fresh breeze. cloudy passing rain. At 4 pm Charles H. Hammond in charge of station."

James Allison followed Hammond and was followed by George Woodman. And throughout the long years of nights, through the fog that frequently enshrouds Chatham, the keepers stayed at their deadly monotonous—and deadly serious—duty of tending the lights.

**Figure 5.4   Chatham Light today (note the absence of the
north tower). Photo by Richard Cooper Kelsey.**

Further changes occurred. In 1923 the north tower of the Twins moved
up the coast to Nauset to replace the Three Sisters (now only one badly
weakened wooden tower). A rotating fourth-order lens replaced the fixed
lens in the south tower, and an incandescent oil vapor (IOV) lamp increased
candlepower to 30,000. The characteristic of the light became group flashing
white (four every thirty seconds).

Then after 1939, when the Coast Guard absorbed the Lighthouse
Service, a 1000-watt electric lamp increased candlepower to 800,000. An
electric motor replaced the old clockworks for turning the lens. This machinery, made in Chelsea in 1802, is still in the light, in case of emergency loss of
power.

Figure 5.5   Chatham Light at night. Courtesy of William E. Joseph.

The spring of 1969 meant a major change for Chatham. The lens and entire lantern room were removed and the lantern rebuilt. Into it went modern 1000-watt aerobeacons. Now the light shows 2.8 million candle-power, with a range of twenty-eight miles. The keeper's double house has become the Chatham Coast Guard Station, and the former lens is on the grounds of the Chatham Historical Society.

CHAPTER

6

Point Gammon Light

Old Light List No. 73 (Obsolete)
41° 36' 33" N, 70° 15' 39' W
Ht. above water: 70 feet
10 lamps; 11 lamps (1843)
Built 1816; closed 1858
Range: 13 miles
Fixed white light
Whitewashed stone tower

*I*n March, 1602, Bartholomew Gosnold (who named Cape Cod for the enormous schools of cod he saw) passed a point of land which he named Point Gilbert in honor of one of his crew, the son of Sir Humphrey Gilbert. The Hyannis harbor entrance is just to the west of this point.

At one time called Fox Point, it is the southern tip of Great Island (now a peninsula). It was part of the land that Yelverton Crowe bought from the Indians in 1639. The rocks of Bishop and Clerks Ledge are some two miles south of the point.

Very early Great Point was the scene of a daring medical experiment. In 1796 Dr. James Hedge of Yarmouth Port, appalled by the number of deaths in a smallpox epidemic, opened an inoculation hospital there. People who had not had the disease received a weak inoculation which produced a mild

**Figure 6.1   Point Gammon tower and dwelling, abandoned.
Courtesy of the Peak family.**

attack and immunity. They would then recuperate at the hospital. Since Dr. Hedge operated the hospital until 1801, he clearly had considerable success.

Winslow Lewis describes the lighthouse in his 1817 *Description of Lighthouses* as:

> *Situated on Point Gammon, at the entrance to Hyannis Harbour, southside of Cape Cod. This light has been recently erected, and was lighted on 21st November 1816. The lantern is elevated 70 feet above the level of the sea, and contains a fixed light.*

The lighthouse and keeper's house were built of local fieldstone, and Samuel Peak moved in with his son John.

The Peaks are an interesting family, with a long lighthouse tradition. John Gilbert Peak was a signer of New Hampshire's Declaration of Independence in 1776. His son John moved to Cape Cod and served as pastor of two churches. Samuel became the first of three generations of keepers. His son

John relieved him when he died in 1824 and served until the light was decommissioned in 1858.

Then he transferred to Bishop and Clerks Light, just offshore, serving there until 1886—a total of sixty-two years. *His* son John spent many years as keeper of the Hyannis Light, just across the harbor. Their descendants live on Lighthouse Lane today.

John Peak's tour of duty at Point Gammon was relatively uneventful. When Lieutenant Carpender inspected the light in 1838, he described it as seventy feet above the sea, twelve miles northwest of Monomoy Light. At that time John's salary was $350 a year. Then, during I.W.P. Lewis's inspection tour of 1845 (see Chapter 2), he signed a statement about the conditions under which he was raising his nine children:

> *. . . dwelling house is extremely leaky, particularly on the east side, where the rain leaks in, so that we always have to move our beds during an easterly rain, and also to mop up buckets of water; . . . The curb of the well is so rotten that we have difficulty obtaining water.*

After the lantern was refitted in 1843 with eleven lamps and fourteen-inch reflectors, things continued quietly. In 1855 Peak's annual Report of Vessels Sighted (required of every keeper) shows: "Schooners—4969; Sloops—1455; Brigs—216; and Steam Boats—4.

That same year, because Bishop and Clerks rocks were a real menace and Point Gammon was not too powerful, a lightship was moored at the rocks. Then in 1858 the light was discontinued, and John became keeper of the new Bishop and Clerks Light, two miles away, in Nantucket Sound.

But history was not through with the lighthouse. Abandoned, the station suffered from vandalism, and several of the buildings were removed. Then in 1872 C. B. Corey bought the whole island (about 600 acres) at a public sale. In 1914 the island changed hands again, when Malcolm Chace bought it, and the Chace family still own it, leasing some property to people who then built there. There is a gatehouse at the only road onto the island.

The stone keeper's house, where John Peak raised his nine children, was dismantled stone by stone about 1935. It was moved to Uncle Ben's Cove on the island, and the stones were used to build a different house. A Mrs. Detweiler used it for many years, and then the Freeman family occupied it. In 1976 Dr. Robert Crowell bought the house. So the old stone house is still sheltering a family after almost two centuries.

The old fieldstone tower, too, has had its life renewed. In 1972 young

**Figure 6.2   The new stone house, built from the old
keeper's house. Courtesy of Rulon Wilcox.**

Arnold Chace thoroughly renovated it and became its first occupant in 114
years. The ground floor served as his kitchen. The middle floor is so small
that, as he said, "I don't know what to do with it. About all one can do is look
out the window up there." The top floor, once the lantern room, was Arnold's
bedroom, with a semi-circular bed, pictures, and books. He lived there for
several summers.

From the lantern room one can easily see Nantucket, thirty miles away,
and seals basking on the rocks below. All year long deer came to feed on the
winter rye that he planted all around the light.

Figure 6.3   The tower today. Courtesy of *Cape Cod Times*.

CHAPTER
7

Race Point Light

Light List No. 460
42° 3.7' N, 70° 14.6' W
Ht. above water: 41 feet
10 lamps; 4th-order Fresnel (1855); aerobeacons (solar-
  powered)
Built 1818; rebuilt 1876
Range: 16 miles
Flashing white ev. 10 seconds (obscured from 220° to 292°)
Horn: 2 blasts ev. 60 seconds
White tower

*R*ace Point and its associated shoals, the dreaded Peaked Hill Bars, are the hard fist of Cape Cod thrust out into the Atlantic. Until the Cape Cod Canal opened in 1914, every ship sailing between Boston and points south had to weather these dangers; failure meant disaster. Thus there were good reasons for Provincetown to petition Congress in 1808 for a lighthouse to mark the point.

The lighthouse was finally built in 1816, the third on the lower Cape. But still some of the Cape's worst wrecks occurred here. One was that of the British frigate *Somerset*, whose bones are still sometimes uncovered by shifting sands. On blockade duty during the Revolution, she hove anchor from Provincetown on October 31, 1778, to intercept a French blockade-

Figure 7.1   First Race Point Light.

runner. After running into thick weather and a gale, she fetched up on the bars. Of her 500 men, over 200 died in the shipwreck.

Luckily for the rest, the gale drove the hulk close enough to the beach that the survivors could be rescued—only to find themselves prisoners of war. The patriotic P'towners marched them all the way to Boston and prison for the duration.

The original tower was of "rubble stone, laid with common lime mortar." The lantern held ten Lewis lamps with thirteen-inch reflectors. The lamps also had Lewis's bottle-green glass "magnifiers," which as one inspector said, only "made a bad light worse." These magnifiers were quite widely used for a time. But at least Lewis's lamps burned less than half as much oil as the old spider lamps of the earlier lighthouses.

His 1817 *Description* described Race Point in great detail, including minute sailing directions for safely entering Provincetown harbor:

This light has been lately erected, and was lit on the 5th of November, 1816. The lantern is elevated 25 feet above the level of the sea, and contains a revolving light on the same principle as Boston light. Vessels coming from sea or round the Cape, will not make the light until it bear S.S.W. the lantern being covered with copper from N.N.E. to E.S.E. to prevent its being taken for Boston light.

While Race Point was not built under Lewis's direction, he took care of its maintenance for many years. The first tower lasted through the storms of sixty years. At that time a keeper's maximum salary was $333.33 a year and use of the land at the station—here pure sand. Just after the Civil War maximum pay was fixed at $600 a year—where it stayed for fifty years.

As often happened, fishing shanties sprang up near the station at Herring Cove because of the fine fishing. P'towners fondly called the settlement "Helltown." There were also extensive salt works (see Chapter 3).

In 1838 the revolving clockwork mechanism was changed to show a flash every minute and a half. And in 1839, to save going the "long way

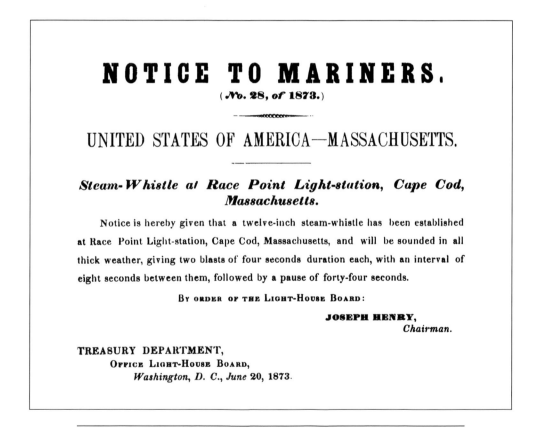

NOTICE TO MARINERS.

(No. 28, of 1873.)

UNITED STATES OF AMERICA—MASSACHUSETTS.

Steam-Whistle at Race Point Light-station, Cape Cod, Massachusetts.

Notice is hereby given that a twelve-inch steam-whistle has been established at Race Point Light-station, Cape Cod, Massachusetts, and will be sounded in all thick weather, giving two blasts of four seconds duration each, with an interval of eight seconds between them, followed by a pause of forty-four seconds.

By order of the Light-House Board:

JOSEPH HENRY,
Chairman.

TREASURY DEPARTMENT,
Office Light-House Board,
Washington, D. C., June 20, 1873.

Figure 7.2   Notice to Mariners, 1873

'round" via the dunes, the town built a dike across Hatch's Harbor, a tidal inlet. Even so, it was a long, slow trek to town for supplies.

Changes continued. In 1852 the government purchased a fog bell for $2500 and installed it. Then in 1893 the Lighthouse Board had the tower rebuilt and shingled and installed a new lantern. In 1874 one of the two keepers' houses was enlarged for the head keeper's family.

The year 1873 was a busy one for Highland and Race Point Lights; they each received mechanical fog signals. Race Point's was a twelve-inch steam whistle, as indicated in the Lighthouse Board's *Notice to Mariners No. 28* of that year. It took a building twelve feet by twenty-four feet to house the cumbersome steam boiler and engine to power the whistle, blowing a distinct, intricate signal.

The reason for the intricate signal is identification. In heavy fog sound waves act most oddly. They bounce off the layers of water particles and seem to shift direction and distance. So each fog signal has to have its own distinctive voice; confusion between signals could lead to disaster.

To indicate how dangerous the Peaked Hill Bars were in the days of sail, more than 100 ships have wrecked there since Provincetown began keeping records. For example, in the so-called Portland Gale of 1888 over 500 lives were lost. Washed ashore was the wreckage of three ships—the *Addie E. Snow*, the *Pentagoet*, and the steamer *Portland*. Only sixty bodies, some fully dressed and some nude, were found. Today bits and pieces of the *Portland* are on display at the Provincetown Monument Museum.

Isaac Small, Marine Reporting Agent at Highland Light, rushed over to help if he could. He describes the scene:

> *As far as the eye could reach on that Sunday morning over the wild sea not the least bit of blue water could be seen for a distance of two miles from shore; the whole ocean was a mass of seething foam; . . . Such was the force of the hurricane of wind that every window pane on the ocean side of our house was blown in. . . . Men exposed to the full force of the storm were blown from their feet and hurled about like blocks of wood.*

In 1876 the old tower, badly weakened, was torn down. Replacing it was a tower of the latest design, of cast iron sheets bolted together and lined with brick. Into the lantern went the 19-5/8-inch diameter Fresnel lens originally supplied in 1855. This lens gave the light its present range of eleven miles. The flashing light became a fixed white light. The Lighthouse Board

**Figure 7.3   Second Race Point Light. Rosenthal photo,
courtesy of Cape Cod Photo Supply.**

reported that the new tower cost $2800; a new garage of 960 square feet cost $5000, and an oil house cost $3000.

To the keepers and their families Race Point must have seemed like the end of the world. Right in front of them was the open ocean, with every storm threatening disaster; behind them was a Sahara of sand, with no human being within call. And each night, from sunset to sunrise exactly the light must burn and be tended; the five-gallon cans of oil manhandled up to the lamp; the watches kept. The keeper's wife, who may have borne him seventeen children (like one wife in Maine), must take over. She is a member of the crew.

In the 1890's the Lighthouse Board reported that there were three keepers and their families at the station. Two families were sharing the larger house, while the other was enlarged to accommodate the head keeper's family.

In 1915, during World War I, William H. Lowther assumed charge of the light after many years aboard the lighthouse tender *Mayflower* and at other light stations. His son, Gerard Lowther, who had a long career in the Coast Guard, recalled with little enthusiasm his childhood trek across two and a half miles of sand to school in Provincetown. Then, in 1920, James Hinckley of

**Figure 7.4   Race Point Light and double keepers' house.
Courtesy of *Cape Cod Times*.**

Barnstable became assistant keeper (the third keeper had been discontinued). When Lowther moved on, Hinckley became head keeper and stayed at
Race Point until his retirement in 1937.

It was Keeper Hinckley who mechanized the arduous trip to town over
the dunes. He soon got tired of lugging supplies by hand; so he got a horse.
But still the trip took seventy-five minutes. Finally, in 1935, he devised what
may well have been the first dune-buggy—a Ford with soft tires—and cut the
trip to a half-hour.

Modernization came slowly to many light stations. For example, it was
1957 before Race Point received electricity. The light source became a 1000-
watt lamp (a spare rotated into position if the first lamp gave out). In 1960–
1961 the Gothic revival keeper's house was demolished and the remaining
house modernized at a cost of $20,000 for a Coast Guard family. The light was
automated in 1978.

Although for some while there was discussion of demolishing all the
structures except the tower, opinion now is that the keeper's house, oil
house, and former fog signal building should be renovated because of the
historical significance of the station.

Billingsgate Island Light

Old Light List No. 59 (obsolete)
41° 51' 36" N, 70° 3' 54" W
Ht. above water: 40 feet
8 lamps; Fresnel lens (1857)
Built 1822; rebuilt 1858
Range: 12 miles
Fixed white light
Red brick tower
Discontinued 1915

Once the glaciers finished shoveling up Cape Cod and the outlying islands from the bottom of the Atlantic, wind and sea continue to this day to revise their shorelines. Especially in winter the nor'easters drive the full force of the Atlantic down upon the forearm of the Cape. The effect is powerful. Isaac Small's ten acres at Highland were only about four when Thoreau visited; now they are about two acres.

Even more striking is the fate of Cape Cod's Atlantis, Billingsgate Island. There was once a thriving community of thirty homes, a school, a try-works for rendering out the oil from blackfish caught in the bay or stranded, and a lighthouse. Today a lonely buoy marks its grave. Deyo's Cape Cod history says that the men of the *Mayflower* in 1620 found an island of sixty acres southwest of Wellfleet. Someone named it "Billingsgate" because the rich fishing reminded him of the great fish market of that name in London.

And it was an accurate name. Those fishing grounds provided the livelihood for men from Dennis to Eastham. The treasures of the sea were there for the taking, whether in gill nets or weirs, with their long nets supported on poles driven into the sand. One saw many weirs fifty years ago; now there are only a few in Nantucket Sound, south of the Cape.

Logs of various keepers record the bonanza hauls. Herman Dill reported in 1874: "A grate cry of Black fish [a species of small whale]. All hands turned out and Drove on Shore about 3 hundred at Truro." Thomas Payne records on May 17, 1878: "Caught ten thousand macerel in the deep water weir at Eastham." And on May 4, 1880: "Another whale was cought near island and sold for $75.00 (30 feet long)." Billingsgate Shoal is today a favorite rendezvous for sport fishermen.

Thanks largely to the efforts of Captain Michael Collins of Wellfleet, Congress authorized the light on May 7, 1822. In June Massachusetts ceded the federal government "a tract of land, not exceeding four acres, which will be found necessary for the Light House. . . ." And on July 9, Elizah Cobb of Brewster sold the United States four acres for $100.

So the lighthouse was built. Brick for it and the keeper's house was ferried over from the mainland. On a granite foundation, the base of the tower was fourteen feet above the water, and the light was "forty feet above the level of the sea," according to Lieutenant Carpender in 1838. He continued: "This is a useful light to this navigation. It is larger, however, than necessary. There are eight lamps in it with 13-1/2-inch reflectors."

Very soon it became obvious that the island was disappearing with every storm. The fishing families began moving themselves and their houses back to Wellfleet as, for some reason, the bay fishing declined. In 1855 the Lighthouse Board reported that "the previous history of this island would indicate that it would be better to build a new lighthouse on screw piles*."

So Congress appropriated $14,000 for a new light in 1856. By 1858 the new construction was completed and the light was lit on September 1, 1858. But for some reason the Lighthouse Board did not follow its own recommendation, and a nearly identical structure was built.

By the 1860's the keepers' tiny domain was drastically reduced. When the bay froze over, their life was cruelly lonely and arduous. Because of wind

---

* The new screw pile design consisted of driving heavy iron legs with large screws at their ends into unstable ground such as sand. The tower and keeper's quarters were built above water around the iron legs.

Figure 8.1   Billingsgate Island Light. Courtesy of William P. Quinn.

and wave, the ice is often a chaotic, impassable mass. Herman Dill's logs tell the story plainly in these excerpts:

1873 January 12   my oil so hard i hav to dip it out

Nov 18   An exceptionally high tide & flooded the tower floor to depth of 2 inches

1875 February 7   it has been very cold here for the last Month and the most ice I ever see in this Rigen We are almost buried up in it. No salt water to be seen from the Island i hav not seen a Living man for over a month no prospect for the better I do get the blues sometimes

Feb 12   I thought the ice was going out but the next day it was back again with Eight vessels in it hard and fast . . . it Rains it Blows it Snows it Hails . . . I have not put my foot on the Mainland for 37 days.

*March 1   There is today 13 Schooners in the ice and one Brig
and there are two Steamers A triing to get them out I
left this Island for the first time in 70 days*

On December 13 the tide "made a clean Sweep through inside . . . there was
from 3 to 5 feet of water." And the next winter (1876) was as bad. Dill's entry
(his last) of March 26 reads: "the very worst storm for the winter was Last
Night." Next day he was found dead in his boat, adrift in the bay.

Five days later Thomas K. Payne reported as keeper; he had been at
Billingsgate from 1860 to 1869. For seventeen years he lived at the lighthouse,
watching the sea eat away at the island:

1881   January 1   I wish all readers of this jornal a Happy New Year

*Oct. 31   I found a finback whale which had run ashore on a
bar NW from this island. J.L.Hopkins and myself
killed and secured him, sold him . . . for $100.*

**Figure 8.2   Billingsgate settlement ca. 1890. Courtesy of Mrs
Irving Henderson.**

*1882   Feb 22   The middle of the Island was flooded five feet of
                    water within fifteen feet of the lighthouse. . . . the
                    island lost thirty feet.*

On June 30, 1884, Captain Payne retired and J. W. Ingals replaced him, serving until 1892.

The Lighthouse Board reported in 1888 that "The sea is rapidly encroaching on this island and threatens the early submergence of the station." To avert disaster they built some 1000 feet of bulkheads and jetties around the site; this action seemed to be effective for a while as sand built up behind the jetties.

The keepers' vigil became even more lonely as the rising water forced the few remaining families to move. By 1898 only a few houses, the lighthouse, and the school remained; the schoolhouse closed when there were only six families left.

Finally the population dwindled to two men—the keeper and the watchman guarding the precious Wellfleet oyster beds in the shallows. By 1915 the station was frequently awash and the tower began to lean. Ropes held the tower in place while men removed the lens and lamp. But the light kept shining from a tripod beacon established at the eastern tip of the remaining island.

The next twenty-seven years record the end of Billingsgate. Dr. Maurice Richardson of Boston bought the islet and when only five acres were left sold it. Soon the sea claimed the rest, and by 1942 the last dry land disappeared.

But Billingsgate may rise again. According to some geologists the island was once part of a land bridge extending to Dennis. Thoreau's Wellfleet

**Figure 8.3   Ruins of the keeper's house. Drawings by David
Grose.**

oysterman told of seeing cedar stumps "as big as cartwheels" on the bottom of the bay.

In view of the rapidity with which Cape Cod readjusts itself to every winter storm (witness the chameleon-like nature of Monomoy Island—a peninsula, one island, or in 1991 two islands), someday the process of erosion might be reversed, and the lush sea meadows that the Puritans found in 1620 could again rise from the sea.

CHAPTER
9

Monomoy Point Light

Old Light List No. 64 (obsolete)
41° 33' 32" N, 69° 59' 38" W
Ht. above water: 33 feet
8 lamps; Fresnel lens (1857)
Built 1823; rebuilt 1849
Range: 11 miles
Fixed white
Red cast iron tower
Discontinued 1923
Repaired 1988

*M*onomoy Point is the visible product of the tidal conflicts between the savage Atlantic Ocean and the gentler Nantucket Sound. Land carved by the sea from Nauset or Chatham becomes part of Monomoy. Bartholomew Gosnold visited here in 1602, and in 1606 Champlain ran afoul of both the shoals and the Indians. The *Mayflower* became so entangled in the shoals and tide rips here on November 9, 1620, that she turned back into Cape Cod Bay. As a result the Pilgrims settled in Plymouth instead of Virginia, their original goal.

In 1729 the ship *George and Ann* landed its passengers on Monomoy after a four-month voyage from Dublin, Ireland. Prevailing winds were against them, and the ship was inadequately supplied for such a long voyage. In addition, over 100 people aboard died of some illness. The passengers

**Figure 9.1   Monomoy Island (Nantucket in the distance).
Airview by Richard Cooper Kelsey.**

were convinced that the captain was starving them to death for their possessions.

A passing Boston-to-New York packet saw the *George and Ann* flying distress signals and investigated. The passengers begged the packet captain, Captain Lothrop, to pilot them to the nearest land, swearing to drown Captain Rymer unless he did so. He agreed and brought them to anchor off Wreck Cove. The passengers went ashore and were taken care of by the Monomoy villagers until they were ready to leave.

They stayed through the winter and then left for Ulster County, New York. Their leader was Charles Clinton, whose descendants included General James Clinton, Vice President George Clinton, and DeWitt Clinton, governor of New York and builder of the Erie Canal.

Early in the eighteenth century a settlement began to grow near the tip of Monomoy, drawn by the seemingly inexhaustible fishing. By 1839 there was a school and a tavern, the Monomoit House. The Chathamites sneeringly called the settlement Whitewash Village because the residents whitewashed their houses instead of painting them.

Long before the building of the lighthouse in 1823, an old couple eked out a living by acting as an aid to navigation. A reporter from *Harper's Magazine* visited the island in 1859 and was told of them by a Monomoyer:

> *Eight years ago [about 1780] we had no lighthouse. But in a shanty . . . lived an old couple who used to answer the purpose pretty well. One or the other of them would come out on the risin' above the water . . . and would pint out the course and marks.*

Periodically Monomoy changes its geographical status; in 1800 it was an island. A few years later it rejoined the mainland, only to become an island later. At the moment (1991) it is two islands, which change in shape and size with every storm.

But whatever its shape, a lighthouse near its southern tip was sorely needed, for it would help the mariner step safely across from Nantucket and on up the coast, staying well outside the dangers of Pollock Rip and Stonehorse and Little Round Shoals.

So on June 3, 1823, the United States bought four acres from Jonah Crowell *et al.* Congress appropriated $3000, and the fifth Cape Cod lighthouse soon rose. The lantern was on the roof of the keeper's house, thirty feet high, with eight lamps. The base of the tower was only three feet above the sea.

Figure 9.2   Desolate Monomoy (Stonehorse Lightship in the distance). Courtesy of William P. Quinn.

In 1838 Lieutenant Carpender reported on his inspection trip to the light, as follows:

> *This memorable light stands on Sandy Point, eight miles from Chatham, a long, low beach that reaches off right into the very heart of the whole coasting navigation, and requires to be lighted, perhaps, more conspicuously than any other. . . . I acquainted myself with the reputation of this light and found it perfectly satisfactory and good. . . . This point of land has received an accession of several hundred yards from the sea, making it probable that, in the course of a few years, . . . it will be advisable to remove this light farther to the southward.*

By 1849 the tower and house were in very poor condition, and so both were rebuilt, the tower in the latest design of cast iron plates lined with brick. In 1857 a fourth-order Fresnel lens gave the light greater range. Unlike many stations, Monomoy was so isolated that between 1841 and 1911 the average

HE COMMUNITY *circling the harbor at Monomoy Point as it appear-*
d in the middle of the nineteenth century.

**Figure 9.3 "Whitewash Village" in the 1850's. Courtesy of
Clair Baisly.**

stay of keepers was only five and a half years. One woman appears in the
record as keeper.

The settlement, on the other hand, fared very well, thanks to the fishing.
At the Powder Hole, wharves, a shipchandlery, and other stores grew up to
serve a large fishing fleet. Lobstering was a rich source of revenue, even when
large lobsters sold for two cents and culls (one-clawed lobsters) for one.

"Wrecking" was also a profitable business. The salvage of vessels driven
ashore provided the winter's fuel supply, as well as ready cash for helping to
refloat a ship not too badly damaged.

But just as the fishing brought prosperity, so it also ruined Whitewash
Village. For some unknown reason, about 1860 the fish left. As a result the
people depending on them left, abandoning most of their houses. A few, like
the Monomoit House, were rafted across the inlet to Chatham. An indication
of the suddenness of the shift is reflected in the Chatham School Committee
report of 1860:

It is hardly to be expected that after this any school can be carried out as the number of people about removing to the main will have the number of students so small as to make it impracticable.

But the lightkeepers and their families stayed on. Asa L. Jones of Harwich kept the light from 1875 to 1886. During the Civil War he had served as a private, corporal, sergeant, and finally second lieutenant of Company A of the Sixth U.S. Colored Troops. His granddaughter, Mrs. E. Justin Hills, has saved the diary of her father, Maro, telling of his life as a boy on Monomoy. Here are some excerpts from 1884, aged nine:

March 31— *Good weather. Papa bound a book. Seven geese came in the pond. Papa tried to shoot them.*

April 6— *Good weather. Papa got three sheldrakes. I scared them for Papa to shoot.*

May 21— *We all went for quahaugs. Lots of Cape Anners [Gloucester fishing boats] came up and it thundered all night.*

May 29— *Windy. I went with Uncle Willie to haul his nets. I went to the station [Life-Saving Station]. Mama and Papa were worried about me.*

November 28— *We came home and left Papa all alone.*

The family would move back to Harwich for school during the winter—and the school year was much shorter then.

Two years later, Maro, now eleven, tells about his last summer at the light:

June 24— *Went to the boathouse to paint dory and to go to the station but a tempest came up and we did not go. After the tempest we went in the dory and I saw Olive. Coming back we stopped at the skate ranch. They have got a new concern there. It is a dryer. In the drying room you cannot live two minutes.*

July 2— *Went to the weir and saw laying on the nets Willie Horton smoking cigarettes.*

July 4—   *Not much of a Fourth of July for me. I never so much as had an explosion of gunpowder.... In the PM the drinkers of Harwich center came after some quahuags for bait to catch black bass.*

July 9—   *My fizic operated (!!)*

August 17—   *Thank the Lord we came off for good. The wind was southwest and Mama was seasick. In the bay were the biggest waves I ever saw.*

Maro Jones, the diarist, became Professor of Latin American Relations and Portuguese at Boston University and later at Pomona College.

Actually Monomoy was hardly deserted in those later days. In 1872 the Life-Saving Service was formalized, augmenting such earlier groups as the Humane Society. Quickly the service built a station two and a half miles north of the lighthouse and another at the southern tip of Monomoy.

Others followed, until the roll call of their names sounds like a tour of Cape Cod's shoreline. Even so, the Humane Society in 1880 still maintained

Figure 9.4   **View from deserted lantern room. Photo by Ben Barnhart, courtesy of *The Cape Codder*.**

Figure 9.5   Monomoy renewed. Airview by Steve Heaslip,
***Cape Cod Times*.**

fifteen lifeboats, mortar stations, and huts of refuge, paying keepers from $5 to $40 a year.

The life-saving crews—heroes to boys like Maro Jones—of six or seven men and a captain manned their stations during the "active season," the ten months beginning on August 1. The keeper (captain) lived at the station and received (in 1890) $900 per year; the surfmen received $65 per month during the season. For this they patrolled the beaches at night and risked their lives to save lives. For example, Captain Marshall N. Eldredge and six surfmen died on March 17, 1902, trying to save five panic-stricken men stranded on the schooner-barge *Wadena*.

From 1871 for the next three years the Lighthouse Board strongly urged that Monomoy Light be upgraded to a second-order (from a fourth) light, saying, "It is considered a matter of the greatest importance that this light should be replaced by one of sufficient power to guide vessels safely through this intricate passage." Nothing was done, however. But in 1882 the tower was painted red!

**Figure 9.6   Gray seals on Monomoy. Photo by Peter Trull,
Cape Cod Museum of Natural History.**

Slowly the life-saving stations were abandoned as their need declined
with the eclipse of sail and creation of the Cape Cod Canal in 1914. In 1923
the light was decommissioned, since the power of Chatham Light was
sufficient to cover the area. Then in 1925 George Dunbar bought the property
at auction for $500, and the only inhabitants were the hunters who banged
away at the teeming bird life.

During World War II Monomoy served as a Navy bombing range, but
even this treatment could not keep the birds away. Then the island (sometimes a peninsula) became a National Wildlife Refuge. Wallace Bailey of the
Massachusetts Audubon Society has counted at least 246 bird species that are
quite frequent, as well as 68 accidental species. A colony of 500 terns settled
there in 1954. He also found 164 species of plant life—from bayberry to
snake-mouth orchid to yarrow.

Today the island (and the light station) are administered by the U.S. Fish
and Wildlife Service. During the summer of 1989 a private contractor
refurbished both the keeper's house and the lighthouse. Since then the Cape

Figure 9.7 "Monomoy Sunset, 1990." Photo by Peter Trull.

Cod Museum of Natural History in Brewster has been leading bird-watching expeditions to Monomoy, staying overnight at the keeper's house. This is one example of the nature recreation (birding, surf-fishing, hiking, photography) allowed.

In January 1990, new inhabitants of Monomoy were discovered. Peter Trull of the Cape Cod Museum of Natural History was leading a bird-watching group when suddenly along the shore they saw a group of gray seal adults and five newborn pups. This fact was of nationwide significance to those interested in natural history; the seals' presence indicates that their breeding range is now farther south than ever before. And this first for Massachusetts provided the seals with an ideal spot, a national wildlife refuge.

Long Point Light

Light List No. 11930
42° 2' N, 70° 9.7' W
Ht. above water: 36 feet
6 lamps; 6th-order Fresnel (1856); 5th order (1875);
    300 mm lantern (solar-powered)
Built 1822; rebuilt 1875
Range: 8 miles
Fixed green
White square tower
Automated 1952
Horn: 1 blast ev. 30 seconds

*T*hree lights mark the tip of the Cape, so dangerous was the route past the ever-changing shoreline and shifting shoals. Race Point (1816) covered the dreaded Peaked Hill Bars; the lighthouse "on Long Point Shoal, southwest entrance to Provincetown harbor," according to the 1857 *List of Light-Houses*, guides vessels into the harbor; Wood End Light (1872) is near the tip of the arm of sand protecting the harbor.

To visualize these lights, hold up your right arm and curl your fingers over. Race Point is at the knuckles; Long Point is at the fingertips; and Wood End is at the last finger joints.

Long Point and Wood End are inaccessible except by boat or along the

**Figure 10.1   First Long Point Light. National Archives
photo.**

beach. But the point's location was such that in 1826 Fifth Auditor Pleasonton
bought four acres out of a Congressional appropriation on May 18, 1826. The
tower and keeper's house cost $15,000 and an oil house and shed cost
another $1000. The light was lit in 1827.

Lieutenant Carpender visited the station in 1838 and wrote:

*It [the lantern] is on the keeper's dwelling, 28 feet above the level of
the sea. . . . This house was in danger from the sea until Government built a ledge, or breakwater, outside of it; since which the
keeper and his family have experienced less anxiety.*

The original oil lamps were replaced in 1856 by a sixth-order lens.

The men of Provincetown to this day are half-aquatic. Very early they
saw a way to use this barren shoal, and by 1818 a settlement began to
develop on Long Point. Given acres of flat sand as well as unlimited salt
water, some built salt works, while others settled for the fishing. Some idea of
the size of the sea salt industry (as it was called) is shown by the fact that in

1812 Cape Cod as a whole produced 100,000 barrels of salts. Provincetown alone had 1,596,150 square feet of vats for evaporating salt water.

As at Billingsgate and Monomoy, the settlement became a community, with some two hundred people living there before 1850. The light station was the center of a busy little village which contained the schoolhouse (later Arnold's hardware store in Provincetown until it burned) and of course numerous windmills to pump seawater into the vats. But during the 1850's the village died out, largely because of the discovery of huge, nearly pure salt deposits near Syracuse, New York.

Especially during southerly storms Long Point Light was increasingly endangered. In 1845 Stephen Pleasonton ordered the light station "close-spiled" (protected with pilings to hold the sand). But in 1873 the Lighthouse Board reported to Congress that:

> *A new keeper's dwelling and tower has become indispensable at this station. . . . The piles on which the present building is supported are decaying, and the entire structure is in danger of being carried off by a heavy storm.*

Figure 10.2   Second Long Point Light (note the Life-Saving Station in the background). Rosenthal photo, courtesy of Cape Cod Photo Supply.

**Figure 10.3   Long Point today (note the solar panels,
installed in 1982). U.S. Coast Guard photo.**

Accordingly Congress appropriated $13,000 on June 23, 1874, for rebuilding
the dwelling and tower and erecting a fog signal. By 1875 the work was done,
as reported that year by the Lighthouse Board:

> *A one-and-a-half story frame dwelling and a brick light tower have
> been erected. . . . A fog-bell tower has been erected . . . and a bell,
> weighing twelve hundred pounds, with a striking machine, has
> been placed on it and put in operation.*

The new tower, with a fifth-order Fresnel lens, was painted brown and showed a fixed white light with a range of eleven miles, according to the *Light List* of January 1, 1887.

During the Civil War the property was assigned to the War Department, to build two coastal defense forts. The doughty citizens of Provincetown promptly named them Fort Useless and Fort Ridiculous. At least, no Confederate cruisers came to call. And for many years the guns helped the town celebrate the Fourth of July.

Keepers at Long Point, as at Monomoy, tended to stay for quite brief periods. Charles Derby served four years (1849–1853), and Hiram Snow (1856–1862) and Herman Smith (1882–1888) served six years. But many of the others put in only a couple of years. After the village left, Long Point must have been a very quiet place indeed.

A plaintive note appears in the Light-House Board report for 1880: "The buildings were repainted and repaired. The keepers have been much annoyed by the stench and flies coming from the fish-oil works near by." So, although the salt works were long gone, still some enterprising Cape Codder was making money at Long Point.

The life of a keeper was difficult enough, but Thomas Chase set some sort of record in 1933. One night the fog signal broke down, and of course a "pea soup" fog rolled in. So he prepared to spend a horrible night hitting the bell by hand every thirty seconds. From 11:00 P.M. to 8:00 A.M. he pulled that bell cord to warn incoming ships.

But his ordeal was not over. The next night in came the fog again. This time, however, he was able to knock off at 2:00 A.M. That morning he went to town to find the needed parts, meanwhile planning how he could work the bell with his legs.

Recent modifications include a reduction in 1927 to 29,000 candle-power, automation of the light in 1952, and in 1982 installation of solar panels so that the light could operate on sunlight and batteries. In addition, the tower (all that remains at the site) received a 300 mm. lantern to replace the fifth-order Fresnel lens. It is not accessible by road but is visible from Provincetown or (close up) by boat.

Nobska (Nobsque) Point Light

Light List No. 14185
41° 30.9′ N, 70° 39.4′ W
Ht. above water: 87 feet
10 lamps; 4th-order lens (1856)
Built 1828 (tower on house)
Rebuilt 1876 (separate tower)
White tower
Range: 16 miles
Flashing white ev. 6 seconds (red sector 263° to 289°)
Horn: 2 blasts ev. 30 seconds
Radio beacon: 291 kHz—NP
Floodlit sunset to sunrise

Nobsque Point Light (as it was called until the 1880's) has a commanding position overlooking Falmouth and Woods Hole harbors. On June 12, 1828, Massachusetts ceded to the United States (with concurrent jurisdiction) four acres on the point for a lighthouse. Then, on July 7, 1828, William and Hannah Lawrence, Andrew Davis, and Elizabeth Lawrence sold four acres for $160 to the government. The deed, in Coast Guard Archives, reads in part:

And we do covenant with the said President of the United States and his Successors . . . That we have good right to sell and convey the same to the President and his Successors, And that we will Warrant and Defend the same premises . . . forever against the lawful claims and demands of all persons.

Accompanying the deed is a copy of the contract for construction of the tower and keeper's house, with the tower on the roof of the house. The entire project, built for $2,249, was completed and approved by September 28, 1828. Details tell us much about the building standards of the day; for instance:

The Dwelling House to be built of brick or stone, thirty-four feet long and twenty wide one story of -8- feet high, divided into two rooms, with an entry between. . . . The walls of the house to be twenty inches thick if of stone, and twelve inches thick if of brick, laid up in lime mortar.

Figure 11.1   First Nobsque Point Light. National Archives photo.

Further specified were a fourteen-by-twelve-foot porch (the kitchen) with a fireplace and "sizeable oven with an iron door, crane trammels and hooks;" a full cellar six feet deep; "a well sufficiently deep to procure good water;" and an outhouse five feet by four, shingled and painted. If good fresh water was not available, a cistern was to be built under the kitchen (porch), with a handpump, into which all the downspouts on the house were to lead—the water supply!

The specifications for the tower were equally interesting. Here are some excerpts:

> *On the centre of the house to be an Octagon Tower, 8 feet in diameter, 16 feet high above the walls of the house. The posts to be 10 inches square, to stand on the beams of the house & well secured together by girths and braces . . . On the top of the tower a Deck 10 feet in diameter formed of 3 inch planks. . . . An Iron Lantern of an octagon form,*

with an iron dome and on its top a "traversing ventilator" as well as a railing around the deck, completed the structure.

Numerous early lights were of this design, one that turned out to be a poor one. The stresses of the tower beams on the house rafters soon produced an extremely leaky roof. More than one keeper complained that every time it rained the whole family had to move their beds. Indeed, the keepers and their families lived hard lives.

The ubiquitous Lieutenant Carpender reported on this light, too, on November 1, 1838:

> *Across Vineyard Sound, at Woods Hole harbor, stands Nobsque light, on the keeper's dwelling, 80 feet above the level of the sea. This light, rivalling in neatness and reputation the last mentioned, consists of . . . six [lamps] in the lower and four in the upper series. I regard the upper lamps as entirely superfluous. This light, though useful, requires to be seen only for a short distance, other lights being near it.*

In the 1840's Peter Daggett was keeper. The Falmouth Historical Society has several documents from that time. For example, his annual report for 1845 of oil used in his ten lamps shows that he used 209 gallons of summer

**Figure 11.2   Present Nobska Point Light. U.S. Coast Guard
airview (date unknown).**

oil and 130 gallons of winter oil*. His comment on the quality of the oil was:
"Very Bad all the Spring Oil and the Winter Not Good."

His December report to Leavitt Thaxter, Superintendent of Light Houses
for Massachusetts, had this to say:

> *This Month Nothing to remark onley have a Great Deal truble to
> Mak the Oil burn.*

> *Everything in Good Order But the Ventilators that wase Put up on
> the Chimneys Is bloon of in the hard Gales It will Lum Smith to alter
> them a Little in the Spring so Thay will Not blow of*

---

* The winter oil was much lighter than the summer, so that it would stay liquid in the unheated
  lantern.

To give some idea of the traffic passing through Vineyard Sound in those days, we have the *Journal of Vessels* which every keeper had to submit monthly. In November, 1864, the count was: Ships—1; Barks—8; Brigs—69; Schooners—652; Sloops—82; Steamers—21. This made a grand total of 833 vessels observed by the keeper. On September 26, 1869, a total of 188 vessels passed the light; 175 were schooners. One wonders if the keepers got any other work done.

The Lighthouse Board reported that by 1875 the keeper's house and tower were in dilapidated condition, and "A fog bell tower has been erected, and a bell with striking machinery placed on it and put into operation." The next year

> *A new cast iron tower and a one-and-a-half story frame dwelling has been erected . . . , the old tower and dwelling having become utterly useless. The expense of the work was defrayed from the general appropriation for the repairs and improvements of lighthouses.*

The original tower was painted white, but now the new tower was painted red. Into it went the fifth-order Fresnel lens of 1856. At the same time a brick oil house and a paint locker were built for $2000—nearly the cost of the house and tower in 1828.

Other improvements occurred. In 1888 the lens was upgraded to fourth-order; it is still there. In 1892 a stone wall five feet thick, five feet high, and 100 feet long was built to protect the site of the bell tower, and in 1899 a covered way (no longer there) connected the dwelling and tower. Then in 1900 a second keeper's house was built, a wood-framed story-and-a-half building; it cost $6000.

An examination of some of the Nobska Point logs reveals much about the spring weather in that area:

1911   5/18   *Moderate E. wind. fog rain. Whistle from 7:30 A.M. till 9 A.M. 1½ hours*

                  5/19   *Moderate East wind fog rain. Whistle from 9.15 A.M. till 10.15 A.M. 1 hr.*

                  5/20   *Moderate Southeast wind & fog. Whistle 12.15 A.M. till 9.30 P.M. 21 hr 15 min. Bell 9:30 P.M. 12 M 2½ hr.*

Figure 11.3   Nobska from the sea. Drawings from *Light House List 1891*.

> *5/21   Moderate Southeast to Southwest wind fog. Bell from 12 M 6.15 A.M. 6 hours 15 min Whistle 6.15 A.M. to 10.45 A.M. 4½ hrs. [Hours of use in four days—37 hours]*

The twenty-second, twenty-eighth, twenty-ninth, and thirtieth were quite foggy too. The bell and whistle received a good workout that month, and the keepers lost a lot of sleep.

Pages and pages of logs are extremely dull reading: weather conditions and the entry "Routine Station work." But here are a few (without the weather) that show some of the events in a keeper's life:

> *4/25/1914   Assistant doin a little in his house on paint in front room, and set one pain of glass in Entry his children broke.*

> *11/27/14   Got a team and took 500 galls from Buoy station to Nobska Point Station today. Keeper went down and loaded same. [A grueling bit of work!]*

> *11/12/17   U.S. Government cruiser is Still upon the Ledge a fleet of 15 boats trying to tower her off but could not move her.*

> *11/17/17   Keeper getting seaweed to cover ground to try and improve soil in same.*

> *11/19/17   U.S. Gunboat was towed of rocks this a.m. Took into Woods Hole*

Figure 11.4   Nobska from the water. Photo September, 1990, by Dr. Richard Sommers.

Improvements have continued. In 1931 a garage was built. In 1937 the new radio beacon began sending the Morse signal "NP" on 324 kilocycles for one minute every six minutes, between signals from Butlers Flats and Cleveland Ledge. Triangulation of these three signals would help a ship find its position. Then in 1948 a steel tower 125 feet high was built for the radio beacon, and the fog signal was changed from a reed horn to a compressed-air operated diaphragm, giving two-second blasts every thirty seconds, audible for five miles.

In 1985 the last Coast Guard keepers left, and the light was automated. This step involved (as at many other stations) installing light-sensitive relays to operate the light. The light source is a 1000-watt tungsten-halogen lamp in the classic fourth-order lens, and there is a back-up lamp that swings into place if the first should fail. Even the fog signal is automated, with a sensor that measures the fog in terms of the moisture in the air.

Today Nobska Point's white tower emits a white flash of light every six seconds, with a red sector covering two nearby shoals. The keeper's house has become the home of the Group Commander, Woods Hole Coast Guard Base.

12

Sandy Neck Light

Old Light List No. 69 (Obsolete)
41° 43' 18" N, 70° 16' 30" W
Ht. above water: 33 feet
10 lamps; later Fresnel lens
Built 1827 (tower on house)
Rebuilt 1857 (separate tower)
Range: 11 miles
Fixed white light, white tower
Disestablished 1921 (replaced by skeleton tower until 1952)
Privately owned today

*S*andy Neck (sometimes called Beach Point) Light is on the tip of the barrier dunes protecting Barnstable harbor and the great marsh behind them. Because Barnstable had a Custom House, shipyards, and heavy traffic of Boston-bound packets and fishermen, Barnstable town meeting ceded two acres to the United States on July 22, 1826. Massachusetts, by act of the General Court, had already ceded four acres (for lights here and at Long Point) on June 20, 1826.

During the next year a brick keeper's house, with a wooden tower on its roof, was built. The light was thirty-three feet above the sea, with ten lamps and reflectors, showing a fixed white light visible twelve miles. The Congressional appropriation had been $3500.

Figure 12.1 Second Sandy Neck Light. National Archives photo.

One of the early keepers was Captain Henry Baxter, who kept the light from 1833 to 1844, after a long career in the coastwise trade. His first log entry on relieving Joseph Nickerson, the first keeper, read: "This day moved my famerly and took possession of the light house at Beach Point, Sandineck, Wind NE, Thick weather." This was on Sunday, December 1, 1833. Other entries reveal some of the problems a keeper faced:

> 12/15/34   *This day a heavy gale from the SW with snow. Came on shore the schooner Enterprise of Mount ? and Capt. Sawyer with two women on board. Got them on shore with much trouble. Capt. Sawyer much frostbit. So ends very cold and the ice making fast the schooner. . . .*

On January 6, 1835, another schooner stranded near the light. His log recorded: "Extream cold most emposable to keep the oil with a lens in the lanton all the time." It was a rugged winter. On February 8 he notes: ". . . the harbor all shut up with ice. The water out of both wells—not able to get any water out of eather." His final entry for 1835 was:

> So ends this year . . . there being 650 schooners and 361 sloops and 2 brigs that has passed in and out over the bar [his yearly report of vessels passing]. Schooner Globe made 33 trips, Sappho 35 trips to Boston.

Another entry notes that a March storm "washed away the bank to the South end of the lighthouse about 70 feet."

Lieutenant Carpender had this to say during his inspection of the light station in 1838:

> This light is on a low, sandy point at the entrance to the harbor, elevated 25 feet [Other sources say 33 or (later) 44 feet.] above the level of the sea. [Of the ten lamps] I recommended suppression of the upper tier. It cannot be that this light requires more lamps than either of the Plymouth [Plymouth—the Gurnet—had two light-houses at that time.]

He continues, pointing out that having a wooden tower on a brick house "is an exceedingly injudicious arrangement, for, if any accident from fire happens to either, both are liable to be destroyed. . . . The premises here are in good order."

Few keepers' logs readily reveal the names of keepers. However, some at Sandy Neck are known. There was, for instance, Jacob S. Howes, who married Eunice Crowell. She was a seventh-generation descendant of John Crow, one of the settlers of Yarmouth in 1639. When Jacob died, she became keeper for two years. Thomas Baxter was another keeper; he married Lucy Hinckley, an ancestor of John Crocker, who owns the logs quoted here. These names—Crowell, Baxter, Hinckley, Crocker—fill numerous pages of today's Cape Cod telephone book.

The elements took their toll of Sandy Neck Light Station. By 1857 the house with its roof tower had to be demolished, and the current brick tower, painted white, was built, with a new Victorian keeper's house. An unusual feature of the construction of the house was insertion of brick walls between the studs of the frame. As a result the house is warm in winter and cool in

**Figure 12.2   Sandy Neck Light today (privately owned).
Airview by Kelsey-Kinnard Photographers, Inc.**

summer. The tower is still there, although the lantern has been removed and the tower capped. It showed a fixed white light.

Then in 1887 the Lighthouse Board reported that:

> *The brick tower, being badly cracked, was strengthened with two iron hoops and six staves. The wooden bulkhead was extensively repaired and filled with sand, and minor repairs were made.*

But well before World War II, in 1931 the lighthouse was disestablished because of large accessions of sand to the tip of Sandy Neck. The optic was moved from the old tower to a steel skeleton tower some two hundred feet closer to the tip. An automatic acetylene light (like those used on large buoys at that time) was installed but was shown only from April to October. During World War II the Coast Guard used the station as a beach patrol headquarters.

In 1952 this light also was discontinued, and the property was declared surplus on June 12, 1953. Edward B. Hinckley and his wife, on December 4, 1954, bought the house and tower for $1551. Their daughter, Lois Hinckley, owns it today.

So ends the story of Sandy Neck Lighthouse and its keepers, who for 104 years served the needs of the port of Barnstable. Although the port is still active, most of the vessels are pleasure craft, with a few fishermen, and not the working sloops and schooners of the old days.

Nauset Beach Light
(or "The Three Sisters")

Light List No. 490
41° 51.6 N, 69° 57.2 W
Ht. above water: 114 feet
10 lamps each tower; 6th-order Fresnel (1858);
*   4th-order (1873)*
Built 1837 (three 15' towers)
Rebuilt 1892; tower from Chatham (1923)
Range: 23 miles
Alternating white/red flashes ev. 10 seconds
Conical tower, upper red, lower white

*A*s with Highland Light, the Boston Marine Society prodded Congress into appropriating funds for "The Three Sisters" at Nauset Beach in Eastham. They formed a committee in 1833 to look into the need for another lighthouse on the outer Cape. Their report recommended building three towers between Highland (one light) and Chatham (two lights). Thus seamen could distinguish between lights. Of course, new lens and revolving technology was available in Europe, but not here.

And so Congress followed Pleasonton's recommendation and voted for "three small light-houses on Nanset [sic] beach, Cape Cod, fifteen feet high, ten thousand dollars." Benjamin H. A. Collins and others sold the United States about five acres at the top of the Nauset cliffs for $150 on September 14, 1837.

Winslow Lewis, the Wellfleet lighthouse expert, was low bidder on the contract. He offered to build a keeper's dwelling, an outhouse, and three lighthouses of brick for $6,549. This offer of course pleased Pleasonton because Lewis was saving $3,451 of the appropriation. The specifications called for the tower walls to be three feet thick at the base and twenty inches at the top.

However, such economy had a price. David Lewis [no relation], the supervisor hired at $2.50 per day, refused to sign off on the job at first because the work was so poorly done. Finally, after prodding by the superintendent in Boston, he did sign. But five years later he wrote the Fifth Auditor that:

> *In laying up the brick-work the masons . . . laid the bricks comprising the interior of the wall entirely at random. . . . I detected the masons several times shoveling in sand instead of mortar. . . . I considered the whole of the work of the meanest character and description.*

This apparently was how Winslow Lewis was able to underbid his competition. Pleasonton's comment on the letter was: "This man will be indicted, and probably punished, for perjury."

Edward Carpender reported on his visit in 1838 in these terms, before the lamps were lit:

> *Nauset beach has always been considered a dangerous place for vessels, and many have been wrecked here. To guard against such disasters seems to be the object of these lights. I cannot, however, think that three lights are necessary. . . . I shall recommend conversion of these lights into a single revolving red light.*

The most serious criticism of the Three Sisters came from I.W.P. Lewis's report of 1842. He chose Nauset as typical of the fraudulent work of contractors (in this case his uncle, Winslow). He wrote that the towers were built on sand with no foundations, that inferior lime went into the mortar, that

Figure 13.1   The "Three Sisters" of Nauset. National Archives photo.

bricks were laid without bonding. He too recommended a single light, flashing every minute and a half.

Often these lights interfered with the important local industry of "mooncussing," as it was called. Local legend tells us that certain people would drive an old white horse, with a lantern tied to his tail, along the cliff to lure trusting seamen onto the beach. There is a similar legend found at Cape Hatteras. When Ralph Waldo Emerson visited Nauset in the 1850's he reported that "Collins, the keeper, told us he found resistance to the project of building a lighthouse on this coast, as it would injure the wrecking business."

In fact, there had long been a most stringent law against such criminal actions. Charles Nordhoff reported in *Harper's Magazine* in 1874 that:

In 1825 it was enacted that "if any person or persons shall hold out or show any false light or lights . . . with the intention to bring any

Figure 13.2   Base of one tower (1987). Courtesy of William P. Quinn.

ship or vessel . . . into danger or distress, every such person . . . shall be guilty of felony, and shall, on conviction, be punished by a fine not exceeding four thousand dollars and . . . confinement to hard labor not exceeding ten years."

But still money could be made from salvage and helping to refloat ships that had stranded at Nauset.

Poor Collins, whose duties earned him enemies, was also the victim of a letter campaign to get him fired. One such letter in the National Archives says, "I feel it a duty to do something to cause removal and as no other person has applied for the situation. I feel prompted to do it myself."

The exposed position of "Nausett," as it was then called, caused frequent repairs. In 1868, for example, ten new window frames went into the keeper's house; a chimney whose ventilator had blown off was extended three feet and braced with iron; and a new sill was put under the bar. And in the next year further major repairs of all sorts were done.

Since the Nauset lights were of minor importance, they had to wait until 1858 to receive sixth-order (the smallest) Fresnel lenses; upgrading to fourth-order did not occur until 1873. And the sea finally claimed the old brick towers (Their bases can sometimes be seen some hundred yards offshore.). Three movable wooden towers, set farther back from the edge of the cliff, began functioning on April 25, 1892. They were seven feet taller than the old towers. Storm porches were added in 1895.

Meanwhile the volume of shipping continued to grow. And wherever one stood on the back shore, a wreck could happen. On December 5, 1893, one of the most dramatic wrecks on Cape Cod occurred. The British bark *Jason*, bound for Boston through a blinding nor'east snowstorm, ran aground so close to the shore that lifelines could reach her.

Yet only one man, Samuel Evans, got ashore because he was washed overboard. The other twenty-six men drowned when the mizzenmast, to which they were clinging, toppled into the boiling sea, and the bark broke in two. Twenty bodies washed up on the beach and were buried in the Wellfleet cemetery.

And ships still keep coming ashore. On March 29, 1984, the Maltese freighter *Eldia*, 471 feet long and in ballast, was driven by hurricane-force winds onto Nauset Beach. A Coast Guard helicopter rescued the twenty-three crewmen. During the next six weeks Clean Harbors, Inc., of Kingston, MA, pumped out 140,000 barrels of oil across the beach, averting a major ecological disaster. Finally, seven weeks after the stranding, tugs pulled the ship off and towed her to a shipyard for salvage.

Meanwhile erosion continued. By 1911 the cliff was within eight yards of the north tower. So the central tower was moved back from the edge, close to the keeper's house. The light was set to flash three times in ten seconds, to commemorate the "Three Sisters." But the tower was so weak that four guy-wires were installed, as a May, 1915 photograph shows.

In 1918 Mrs. Helen M. Cummings of North Eastham was high bidder at an auction of the two end towers. Her bid was $3.50. They became part of a summer cottage for many years. Finally, in 1965, the National Park Service bought the towers from John Cummings, son of the original buyer.

The middle tower (which became known as "The Beacon") served until 1923. Then the northern tower of the "Chatham Twins" was dismantled and reassembled at Nauset, and the old fourth-order lens (made in France by Barbier and Fenester) moved into the new lantern. In 1939 it was replaced by twin aerobeacons, and it is on display at the Salt Pond Visitor Center in

Figure 13.3   Wreck of the bark *Jason*, 1893. Rosenthal photo, courtesy of Cape Cod Photo Supply.

Figure 13.4   Maltese freighter *Eldia* aground, 1984. Airview by Richard Cooper Kelsey.

Figure 13.5   Two of the towers as part of the Cummings cottage. Courtesy of the Cape Cod National Seashore.

Figure 13.6   The north tower from Chatham replaces the "Three Sisters" (1923). Photo by Richard Cooper Kelsey.

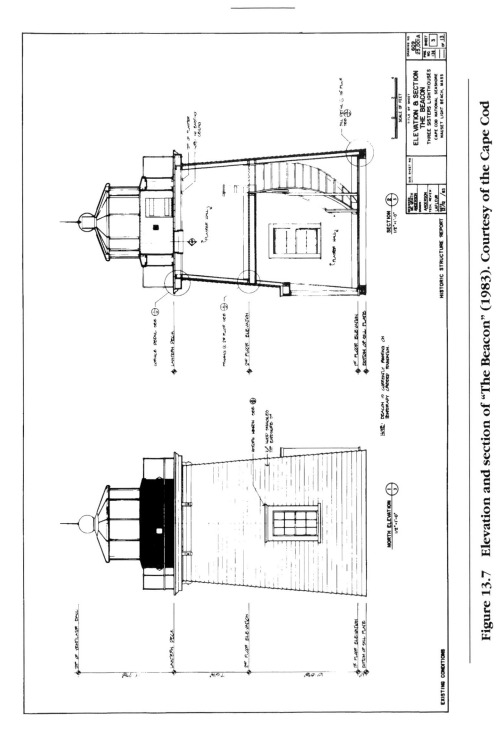

Figure 13.7   Elevation and section of "The Beacon" (1983). Courtesy of the Cape Cod National Seashore.

Eastham. At the same time the keeper's house was moved onto a new walk-in cellar.

That same year (1923) Albert Hall bought the middle tower and moved it, making it part of another summer cottage. Finally Albert's son Harold sold his cottage to the National Park Service, and in the summer of 1983 the additions were removed, so that the tower stood alone.

In 1990 the Park Service moved all three towers to a site off Cable Road in Eastham and placed them exactly the 150 feet apart that they originally stood. They refurbished them, to be open to the public.

Mayo's Beach Light

Old Light List No. 58 (Obsolete)
41° 55' 48" N, 70° 1' 42" W
Ht. above water: 26 feet
3 lamps; Fresnel lens (1856)
Built 1838 (tower on house)
Rebuilt 1881 (separate tower)
Range: 6 miles
Fixed white light
Disestablished 1922
Tower razed ca. 1939
House privately owned today

Wellfleet and Provincetown have the two largest and safest harbors on the inside coast of Cape Cod. Both have been centers of the fishing industry for generations and so were prime candidates for lighthouses. Provincetown already had Race Point and Long Point Lights; now it was Wellfleet's turn.

So on September 22, 1837, Justin Taylor, shoemaker, and his wife Pauline sold the government a rectangular piece of land 175 feet by 79 feet for $80. During the next two years Congress appropriated a total of $3000 "to enable the Secretary of the Treasury to provide, by contract, for building a light-house on Mayo Beach, in Wellfleet Bay, in the state of Massachusetts."

**Figure 14.1   First Mayo's Beach Light. National Archives
photo.**

The contract, completed for $2819.18, provided a keeper's house with
the tower and lantern projecting from the roof. This design, as we have
already seen, caused the keepers' families a great deal of misery, since the
roof soon began to leak because of the stresses placed on the roof rafters and
roof itself.

During his tour of inspection in 1838 Lieutenant Carpender reported
scornfully on the location of the lighthouse:

> *I was surprised to find a light-house building on Mayo's beach . . .
> and wrote to you in hopes of arresting the work. This harbor is but
> four miles long, and when vessels get within Billingsgate light they are
> as safe as they can be in any part of the harbor. . . . Some venerable
> old fishermen and pilots belonging to the place, whom I consulted,
> declared their opinion openly and publicly against the light; and
> elsewhere on the cape . . . it raised a smile. . . . But, according to my
> judgment, it should be entirely suppressed.*

According to Carpender, the tower showed a fixed white light, forty feet above the sea, visible twelve miles, from three lamps with fourteen-inch reflectors. Surprisingly, his figures disagree with those of the light list of the time.

Joseph Holbrook of Mayo's Beach became embroiled in 1848 in the vicious political battle between two Cape Cod newspapers. Amos Otis of the *Yarmouth Register* inspired an item appearing in the *Boston Atlas* on November 30, 1848:

> *We have had in our possession for several days, some interesting facts relative to the manner in which a leading Democrat on Cape Cod derives a certain amount of "Black Mail" from the Locofoco Light House Keepers. . . . He claims this pay, we understand, on the ground that he procured the appointments to be made, and thro' his influence the incumbents are kept in. Perhaps the editor of the Barnstable Patriot can tell us something about the matter.*

S. B. Phinney, editor of the *Barnstable Patriot*, wrote Holbrook asking for the facts about $40 Holbrook had paid him in 1846. Holbrook explained that he had asked Phinney to help him refute claims of a smear campaign against him (Keepers' jobs were highly prized at that time.). The editor had even gone to Washington in his behalf, and the $40 was all that Holbrook could afford to reimburse Phinney.

Phinney then published a bitter diatribe against Otis, pointing out that he had produced no evidence to back up the charge. He ended it:

> *Such is a specimen of the "fairness" of the prowling, pimping, lying genius who is Cashier of the Barnstable Bank! Did we not correctly denominate that Bank, last week, as a "scandal-monger's stall?"*

Soon after the 1852 Congressional overhaul of the system and creation of the Lighthouse Board, in 1856 and 1857 Mayo's Beach and fifteen other lights in the district received new Fresnel lenses and much-improved lamps.

Joseph Holbrook managed to hold onto his job until the end of the Civil War, when he was ousted to make way for William N. Atwood. But he did not give up easily. On May 29, 1865, Lighthouse Inspector John Marston wrote a strong letter of support to Rear Admiral Shubrick, saying in part:

> *Mr. H. Is a most estimable, intelligent man, of whom I have had no complaints. He has had three sons in the war . . . [one] was killed,*

leaving three orphan children to Mr. Holbrook to support. I cannot but think if these circomstances had been known to the Board [the Lighthouse Board], Mr. H. would not have been removed.

But the letter was too late. On May 9, 1865, the Superintendent of Lights in Boston had sent to Washington Atwood's oath of office and receipt for supplies.

William Atwood also had a good claim on compassionate grounds. He had lost an arm at Fredericksburg, Virginia, on December 23, 1864. A Wellfleet boy, he had grown up going to sea and enlisted at the age of forty in Company K, 12th Regiment, Massachusetts Infantry. Soon after his discharge on February 9, 1863, he married Sarah Cleverly. Incapacitated for going to sea, he applied for the Mayo's Beach job.

His appointment was effective on April 1, 1865, at a salary of $350 per year; two years later it was raised to $500 in the general improvement of salaries by the Lighthouse Board.

Aside from routine repairs, the years went by quietly at Mayo's Beach. Between 1865 and 1873 the Atwoods had five children: James, John, Robert, Jennie, and Lizzie, who died at five months. One example of the relatively minor repairs comes from the Board's report of 1868:

63. Mayo's Beach.—Leak in tower stopped with paint cement; tower and exterior trimmings repainted; glass set where required; illuminating apparatus examined and adjusted; burners repaired; cooking stove and chest of tools supplied.

William Atwood died on June 14, 1876, leaving his widow with four small children. Compassionately, the Lighthouse Board named Sarah temporary keeper in July and permanent keeper on August 26, 1876. A major reason for the decision was that because the lantern was on the roof of the house she could tend the light without going outside. She remained as keeper until her resignation on May 7, 1891—twenty-six years living at the light station.

Her youngest daughter, Jennie, had grown up and married Captain Thomas Bryne, going to sea with him. So Sara resigned and moved uptown to her house on East Commercial Street. Her successor was James Smith of Provincetown, appointed on May 7, 1891.

As a boy Earl Rich of Wellfleet remembers "Aunt Sarah" Atwood, who lived next door to his family. Independent, she had a flock of hens, and her vegetable garden kept her well supplied; not a square inch of the yard was wasted. She died, aged eighty-three, on November 20, 1920.

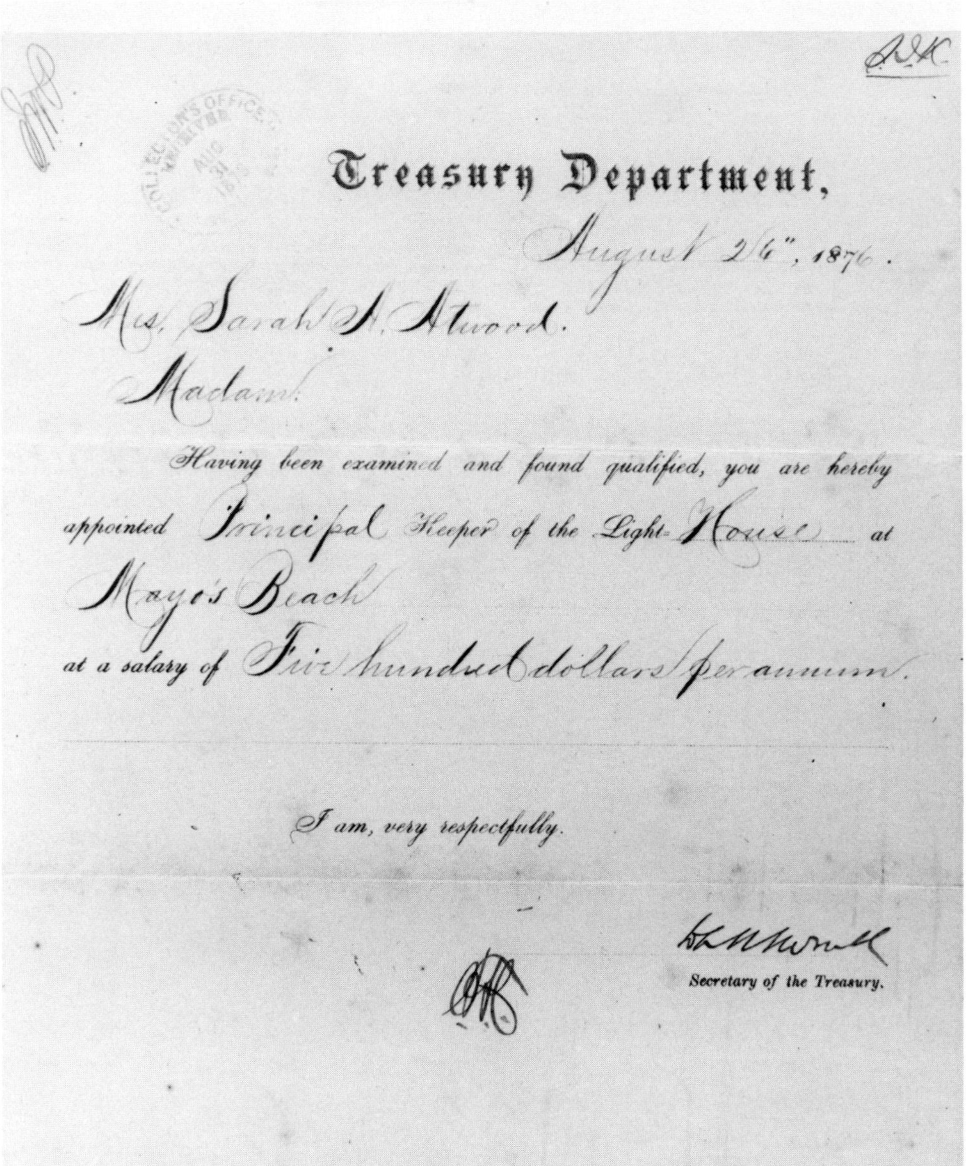

Treasury Department,

August 26", 1876.

Mrs. Sarah A. Atwood.

Madam:

Having been examined and found qualified, you are hereby appointed Principal Keeper of the Light-House at Mayo's Beach at a salary of Five hundred dollars per annum.

I am, very respectfully.

Secretary of the Treasury.

Figure 14.2 Sara Atwood's commission. Courtesy of Wellfleet Historical Society.

**Figure 14.3   The second Mayo's Beach Light. Rosenthal
photo. Courtesy of Cape Cod Photo Supply.**

But, even in its protected position at the head of the harbor, the station suffered from continuing erosion from storms. By 1878 the Board recommended rebuilding of the house, and during 1880 and 1881 the new, larger story-and-a-half house and separate tower of iron plates (like Chatham's last towers) rose on the site.

On an inspection during rebuilding, Commander Winfield Scott Schley wrote Admiral Shubrick, pointing out a serious problem:

I observed . . . that the lantern top of the new Tower, building on Mayo's beach, was partially intercepted by the top of the roof of the old dwelling, behind which it is placed. When the light is shifted to the New Tower it will be necessary to tear away, not only the old Tower, but also the roof of that dwelling in order that the new light may be unobstructed.

New orders came from Washington, and "the old dilapidated structures [were] torn down."

Figure 14.4   The keeper's house today (note the "ginger-bread" eaves). Courtesy of Harry Parkington, owner.

Even four miles inside the harbor, the station continued to need further efforts to shore up the property. In 1889 the Board reported that over one hundred feet of plank bulkhead had to be replaced. In 1895 fifty loads of loam were spread around the house to keep it from being undermined. And in November 1898, a storm carried away the entire bulkhead and the new soil, requiring replacement.

The final years of the light were quiet. In 1907 an oil house for the flammable kerosene now used was added. Finally, on March 10, 1922, the light was discontinued, and the last keeper retired. Then, in 1923, the property was auctioned off by sealed bids. On August 1, 1923, Merle A. Higgins of Provincetown won with a bid of $3605 and received a deed specifying "the same land conveyed to the United States by Juston Taylor, September 22, 1837."

Since then the house has passed through many hands and is still lived in and enjoyed. Its history can be traced in the Barnstable Registry of Deeds. Ralph Hopkins bought it in 1925 and four years later sold it to Captain Harry Capron. During their ownership (about 1939 according to the Wellfleet Historical Society) the Caprons had the tower torn down. Its cement foundation is still visible just outside the porch overlooking the harbor. They occupied the house until 1980, when the Poltorak family bought it. Finally, on April 1, 1986, Kathleen and Harry Parkington acquired it and have lovingly restored it to its original shining condition.

Wing's Neck Light

Old Light List No. 92 (Obsolete)
41° 40' 47" N, 70° 39' 41' W
Ht. above water: 44 feet
8 lamps; Fresnel lens (1856)
Built 1849 (tower on house)
Rebuilt 1890 (separate tower and house)
Range: 10 miles
Fixed white light
Disestablished 1946
Privately owned today

*T*he year 1849 was a good year for lighthouses on Cape Cod. Three were built: at Wing's Neck in Pocasset, at Hyannis harbor and at the Pamet (or Parmet) River in Truro.

There was heavy traffic in Buzzards Bay from Wareham, from Sandwich harbor, and from the Pocasset Iron Works. Consequently, on recommendation, Stephen Pleasonton requested funds for a light station on Wing's Neck, which projects out into Buzzards Bay. Much later, of course, the site represented the approach to the Cape Cod Canal, opened in 1914.

First, on March 13, 1849, George and Nancy Ellis sold 9.57 acres to the United States for $250. John Vina received the building contract in May, and by August 14 he had erected a stone keeper's dwelling, with a red roof and

**Figure 15.1   First Wing's Neck Light. Courtesy of Bourne
Historical Society.**

with the tower and lantern protruding from it, for $3251. Edward D. Lawrence
became the first keeper.

But not for long. Given the politics of the service at that time, he was
ousted in 1854 by Samuel Barlow. The Sandwich *Register* had this comment
to make:

> *Mr. Lawrence was a faithful, capable man and was appointed at
> the time the Lighthouse was built. . . . His crime consisted in Having
> been appointed by the Whigs.*

Eleven years later, after keepers Barlow, Weight, and King, Lawrence
returned to the light, and he stayed in command until 1887. In 1878 the tower
was destroyed by fire, and the Lighthouse Board reported that:

> *There is no tower at this station. The lantern is on top of the
> dwelling; the roof has been crushed by the weight. A new tower is
> required, and the dwelling should be extensively repaired. The
> estimated cost is $5000.*

**Figure 15.2   Second Wing's Neck Light. Airview courtesy of
U.S. Corps of Engineers, Buzzards Bay, Mass.**

However, after some repairs the keeper's house and lantern continued to serve until 1890. Then the stone house was demolished and a "frame dwelling 28 × 31 feet" was built on the same foundation ("Waste not, want not!"). A framed pyramidal tower nearby received the old lantern and the Fresnel lens of 1856. At the same time the contractor built a walkway between the house and the tower.

After Edward Lawrence's twenty-seven years, his replacement lasted twenty-five days. Albert Gifford relieved him and served twenty-one years, dying at his post in October 1908. Edward Nickerson, town undertaker, describes that terrible night:

> *I hitched up my old nag and drove down there. Mrs. Gifford was alone [and] as I worked on the body, she carried on through that beastly, cold, foggy night, tending the light and clocking the fog bell . . . sticking to her husband's responsible job.*

**Figure 15.3　Wing's Neck Light. Photo by Dr. Richard
Sommers, January 1991.**

And she stayed on the job for two weeks before being relieved by Wallace
Eldredge and his wife Louise.

The Eldredges spent thirteen years at Wing's Neck before he retired in
1921, after thirty-three years in the Lighthouse Service. His story, in brief,
reveals something of the quality of these men. Son of a whaler, he was born
on a Nantucket farm in 1856. Married at twenty to one of the belles of the
town, Louise Joy, he became a carpenter.

His next career was that of a travelling salesman, selling cutlery all over
the Middle West. He was in Missouri when Jesse James was gunned down.
Soon Frank James gave himself up, and Eldredge "had a long talk with him"
in jail.

> *He was a handsome gentlemanly appearing fellow, finely set up
> and well dressed. Nobody would have surmised . . . that he was one
> of the bandits who had terrified the whole West.*

Drifting back to Nantucket, he became a lighthouse keeper almost by accident. His brother-in-law, who was high in Democratic politics, offered him the post at Sankaty Head. He accepted readily, and so began his long career in the Lighthouse Service.

His greatest moment, perhaps, occurred during President Harding's visit to Cape Cod aboard the Presidential yacht *Mayflower*. The weather was so foul that the yacht anchored off the Neck, and in the morning the Eldredges gave the President their "twenty-one-gun salute" on the station's fog bell. They repeated it when the President left on the following Sunday. During his time at Wing's Neck, he earned five Efficiency Gold Stars, awarded by the service for superior performance.

After the Cape Cod Canal opened in 1914, Mrs. Eldredge was for seven years the day dispatcher for the canal. She would telephone news of all eastbound ship arrivals to the canal office in Buzzards Bay, where the canal actually started. She also handled weather signals for the Coast Guard.

Following the Eldredges were the Howard brothers, George and William. They were responsible for many rescues in Buzzards Bay. For example, in eight months in 1932 they saved eight lives, and during Captain William's career he saved at least thirty-seven lives.

Captain George Howard (the "captain" is an honorary title often given keepers) illustrates the longevity of many keepers. He began his career on Thatcher's Island in Rockport in 1907. Two years later he was promoted to keeper at Duxbury Pier, at twenty-three the youngest head keeper in the service. Next he went to Tarpaulin Cove on Naushon Island for two years before moving to the Ipswich station. Four years later he enlisted and served during World War I, returning to Wing's Neck. He completed thirty years of service on May 1, 1937.

Changes at the light continued. When the canal opened, the oil lamp was changed to a vapor lamp. Then, in 1922, the keeper's dwelling from the closed Mattapoisett station was moved by barge across the bay, to become the assistant keeper's house. In 1943 a steel skeleton tower for the Army Corps of Engineers was erected on land ceded to the corps. It now holds approach radar for control of ship movements in the canal.

With construction of Cleveland Ledge Light (1941) and Buzzards Bay Light (1961), Wing's Neck was considered non-essential. The property was sold to Frank and Irene Flanagan in 1947 for $15,911, highest bid of sixteen for the property. Mrs. Flanagan still lives in the keeper's house, while the assistant's house is owned by her brother. Other lots on the acreage are owned by close friends.

South Hyannis Light

Old Light List No. 74 (obsolete)
41° 38' N, 70° 18' W
Ht. above water: 36 feet
10 lamps; Fresnel lens (1856)
Built 1849
Range: 8 miles
Fixed white light
Disestablished 1929
Privately owned today

*T*he South Hyannis Lighthouse began as a privately-owned light. Daniel Snow Hallett decided that there was a need for one to guide the heavy traffic in and out of Hyannis. He moved a one-room shack to the shore and cut a window in the loft, where he displayed an old lamp and reflector borrowed from Point Gammon.

His son, Daniel Bunker Hallett, who became a Boston banker, recalls his part in tending that primitive lighthouse:

> *As a boy of 10 or 12 I often used to walk . . . two miles to the harbor light . . . to light the lamp and remain all night alone, with only my dog Pilot for company; then return home in the morning to get breakfast and go to school.*

**Figure 16.1   First South Hyannis Light Station, ca. 1850.
National Archives photo.**

After some prodding, Congress on August 14, 1848, appropriated $2000 for a small harbor light at Hyannis. Fifth Auditor Pleasonton reported to Congress that:

With much difficulty a small piece of land was purchased, a small tower erected and fitted up with lamps and reflectors, for the sum appropriated. A man has been employed to attend it . . . at the rate of fifteen dollars per month.

The light was lit by Daniel Snow Hallett, the first keeper, on May 1, 1849. The tower was known as the "Bug Light" by the neighbors because it was so short. It showed a fixed white light with a red sector covering the Hyannis breakwater and Southwest Shoal. Large tallow candles were kept for emergency use.

To further illustrate the degree to which politics entered into the service, that same year James Bearse became keeper under President Fillmore. Then,

**Figure 16.2   Light with remodeled lantern. Courtesy of the
Peak family.**

when President Pierce was elected, Almoran Hallett, Daniel's brother, was
named. Franklin Baker was appointed in 1861, and in 1871 John Lothrop of
Hyannis. On his death in 1878 his son Alonzo became keeper until 1899; then
John Peak, formerly of Point Gammon and Bishop and Clerks, was named. Ill
health in 1915 forced Peak to resign, and Waldo Leighton became keeper, to
stay until June 30, 1929, when the light was decommissioned.

Waldo Leighton had previously been at Race Point with his three sons,
Harvard, Edgar, and Robert. The boys were delighted with the move to
Hyannis from one of the most isolated stations on Cape Cod. Harvard, now in
his eighties, described his new home as:

> *a wonderful location, a nice place to live, a picturesque site over-
> looking the whole bay. . . . Our home was a charming two-story
> dwelling with a full cellar and an outhouse. It had no electricity or
> running water. Although it was as primitive as the one in
> Provincetown, it was not so isolated.*

Meanwhile on September 30, 1850, Congress appropriated $800 "for a dwelling-house for the keeper." In 1856 the tower received its small Fresnel lens. In those days the railroad line ran right down onto the wharf beyond the light. Alonzo Lothrop kept a record of the business at the wharf. He notes:

1882—Discharged 6,000 tons of coal; 1,250,000 feet lumber; 100,000 bushels grain; 4,000 barrels fish. Arrived in harbor, 1,400 schooners, 100 steamers.

A few years later the War Department report on Hyannis harbor traffic indicated:

1893—Discharged 14,750 tons coal and 53,348 bushels grain to H.B. Chase and Sons and Messrs. Hull and Burt; 20 cargoes lumber for Sears and Hinckley yards; 3,000 barrels fresh fish received and shipped by rail. Value of imports, $557,700; exports. $102,925.

Clearly the population of Cape Cod had grown considerably in those eleven years. And also clearly the Cape had a very heavy negative balance of trade with the rest of the world.

Hyannis harbor was a busy place in the nineteenth century. The wharf had moorings for half a dozen ships; the daily Nantucket steamer landed there; Heman Chase and Daniel Merchant owned a shipchandlery and grocery and ran a packet line. A grain and coal business, a fish house, and a lumber yard were also located at the wharf.

Then in 1885 a wooden tower, twenty feet tall, was built at the end of the wharf to serve with the lighthouse as a range for ships entering. The light was an oil lamp mounted on an iron base, which was hoisted to the top of the tower by a chain.

But the primitive design of the beacon often caused difficulty because the light would blow out in storms. So in 1886 the Lighthouse Board rebuilt the beacon and supplied it with a new lamp to solve the problem. In 1889 an oil house and summer kitchen were added to the keeper's dwelling, and the barn, covered way to the light, and the fence were repaired.

When Captain John Peak was at the light he had a running battle with the railroad, because they would often leave freight cars next to the beacon, blocking it. He would have to go down to the wharf and argue with the railroad to persuade them to move the cars.

Waldo Leighton, the last keeper of the light, shut down the lamp for the last time on June 30, 1929, and transferred to Nobska Point Light in Woods Hole. The government replaced the range light at the end of the wharf with an acetylene gas beacon of 230 candlepower and removed the entire lantern from the tower, capping it.

Declared surplus, the property was sold at auction to a Miss Stevenson for $7,777.77. Since then it has had many owners: David McCargo, who later bought the railroad wharf; Judge Paul M. Swift; Sebastiano Volpe, who was the contractor building Cape Cod Community College in the late 1960's; Dorothy Gilliland, who owned Gosnold Village in Hyannis; Eugene Mahoney, an off-Cape Developer; David Ives of WGBH; and the present owners, Janice Hyland and Alan Granby, owners of the Carriage House marine antiques shop in Brewster.

Figure 16.3 The light station as a private home. Courtesy of the Peak family.

**Figure 16.4   The tower and dwelling today, from the water
(note the new enlarged lantern room, used as a sitting
room). Photo by Dr. Richard Sommers, 1990.**

Pamet (Parmet) Light

Old Light List No. 57 (Obsolete)
No. part of Pamet harbor, south end of salt works
Ht. above water: 31 feet
1 lamp with 21" reflector
Built 1849 (tower on keeper's house)
Range: 6 miles
Fixed red light
Disestablished 1856
Property sold 1857 (no record of buyer in Archives)

*P*amet Light (or Parmet, as the old-timers called it even as late as 1927) was built at the mouth of the tiny Pamet River in Truro, facing Cape Cod Bay. This is the mystery light of Cape Cod, for almost nothing is known about it. Even the material in the National Archives is quite sparse. For example, a card file lists twenty pieces of official correspondence. But all except one letter burned in a fire years ago at the Archives.

Shebnah Rich's *Truro, Cape Cod* describes the thriving little harbor there:

Here were wharves covered with stores and sheds; crowded with vessels. Forty-nine were hauled up one winter. . . . Here was a shipyard. . . . Much of the timber was cut in town and drawn to the

*yard, all of which kept the people at work. . . . Three packets were
employed carrying fish to Boston, . . . besides several traders and
coasters to New York and other points. . . . Salt manufactured along
the shore . . . was brought down to the wharves in scows to a ready
market. . . . In 1849 Government built a lighthouse on Snow's
Beach, which was discontinued after a few years. . . . The real
occasion, probably, for the removal, was the decline of business. . . .*

That year (1849) the steamer *Cambria* from Liverpool grounded on the
Atlantic side of the Cape. Tugs were able to pull her off without much
trouble. The English passengers went ashore and thought the view "the most
delightsome they had seen." And the Wellfleet oysterman later told Thoreau
that the ladies "played pranks with his scoop-net in the pond."

One mystery is that even the location of the light is in question. The 1848
Coast Survey (and corrections to 1909) puts the light several miles farther
north, above the entrance to the so-called north branch of the river, which is
little more than a creek. Its indicated location is high on Corn Hill, but an 1858
map puts it on Snow's Beach at the main mouth of the river.

On May 11, 1849, Jane Snow, executrix for her father's estate, sold the
United States three-quarters of an acre of land for $125. Congress had already
appropriated $5000. For some reason, despite previous bad experiences with
the design, the Lighthouse Establishment chose to build another saltbox with
the tower projecting from the roof.

Then on May 8, 1849, P. Greeley, Jr., Superintendent of Lights in Boston,
published specifications for the house and light tower:

*Building hard brick laid in best Rosendale cement, thirty-six feet by
eighteen; cellar under the whole house, six feet in the clear under
the flooring joists; cellar walls one foot thick, floor paved with hard
brick; . . . walls of the house one foot thick, carried up nine feet
above the cellar walls. . .; house divided in two rooms, entry between, eight feet wide; stairs to lead into attic; . . . attic divided into
two chambers; . . . In the centre of the building to be an octagon
tower, eight feet in diameter at the corners; . . . stairs to lead from
the attic floor to the lantern.*

*On the top of the tower to be a wrought iron lantern, sufficient
height and diameter to contain six lights in each octagon, 16 × 24
inches; on the top of the dome a traversing ventilator and vane,
covered with copper. . . .*

The whole to be done in a workmanlike manner, . . . and completed on or before the first day of August next.

Then more confusion occurs. The one surviving letter in the Archives is from a John Donohoo, of Havre de Grace, Maryland, dated June 5, 1852. He quotes a price of $4400 for the job (saving the government $600), and "if the whole of said work is not approved by the Inspector to be done in a faithful and workmanlike manner I will not ask one cent for it." But the light station had been built three years before.

The 1854 *List of Lights* gives 1849 as the date of establishment, describing the light as being fixed red, thirty-one feet above the sea. This is further evidence of the lower location of the light at the harbor, because of the hilly topography of the other site. The lantern on top of the keeper's dwelling had a single lamp with a twenty-one inch reflector.

Another mystery concerns the identity of the keepers of the light. According to his great-granddaughter Natalie Rich Foster of Truro and Florida, and several other sources, Thomas Peterson (1822–1863) was the sole keeper of Pamet Light. After its disestablishment in 1856 (she says 1853) he joined the Navy in 1862 and became captain of the gunboat *Diana*. The *New Orleans Era* reported that he took his command too far up a southern river and was ambushed at close range by Confederate cannon. The story ends:

It was at this moment that Capt Peterson, while standing on the deck, . . . received a ball in his breast, which prostrated him to the deck. His only words were "I am a dead man." All the other officers were killed or badly wounded as were many of the crew from cannon fire sixty feet away.

Again there is more confusion. The National Archives' list of light-keepers gives the names of three other men. James Davis was appointed on July 27, 1849, at a salary of $350 per year (later reduced to $300). Reuben Burdett succeeded him on February 14, 1852, at $300. Finally, John Kenney became keeper on May 4, 1853, at $300 and served until 1856, when he moved to Highland Light for two years. There is no mention of Thomas Peterson in the record.

The light was discontinued on November 20, 1856, and the government sold the property the next year. Apparently because of the fire, the Archives have no record of the actual sale or the buyer. And to date there is no known photograph of the lighthouse.

Much later, on August 27, 1927, Charles W. Snow, a Truro contractor, wrote to Captain Easton, Lighthouse Inspector in Boston. He wanted to know about the status of the old lighthouse property:

A good many years ago there was a light house at Parmet River, Truro Mass, will you kindly favor me by looking up the records of that peice of land, it was bought of a Captain Lewis Lombard, . . . a few years ago I bought that estate, this peice of land . . . is right in the middle of my property, I am wondering if it was turned back to the estate or if the United States still ownes it, and if it does is there any way I can get it as I want to get this straightened out, I am getting along in years. So will you kindly let me know the facts, and if any expence please let me know also.

J. J. Conway, Acting Commissioner of Lighthouses, replied on September 9, 1927, that the property was sold in 1857 or 1858. But because of the fire there is no information as to the buyer. He suggested searching in the Barnstable County records.

And that is the extent of the information on "Parmet" Light, together with its mysteries. Perhaps this brief history will encourage someone to solve the mysteries and add more to the history.

Bass River Light

Light List No. 13273
41° 39' 04" N, 70° 10' 10" W
Ht. above water: 44 feet
Fresnel lens; modern optic (1989)
Built 1855
Range: 12 miles
Flashing white every 6 seconds
Tower on large white house
Disestablished 1880 and 1914
Sold at auction 1915
Reestablished; privately operated May 1 to Oct. 31, 1989

*T*here was considerable controversy over whether or not to place a lighthouse at the mouth of Bass River (separating the south sides of Dennis and Yarmouth). The officer who first surveyed the area deemed a light unnecessary. But masters of the many ships using the river had each been contributing twenty-five cents a month for oil for a private light on Wrinkle Point. This primitive light was a lantern placed in the attic window of a house. They asked the Lighthouse Board to reconsider.

The Board did, and Congress appropriated $4000 in 1850 for a lighthouse on the new jetty on the east side of the river. But the site was unsuitable, and a new location was chosen.

**Figure 18.1   Bass River Light. Courtesy of Mrs. Irving
Henderson.**

Finally, in 1854, oxen dragged the building materials several miles over
marshes and dunes. Soon a white one-and-a-half-story keeper's house, with
the tower on the roof, was built. A fifth-order Fresnel lens displayed a fixed
white light with a range of eight miles. It was first lighted on April 30, 1855.

Warren Crowell became the first keeper. In December, 1863, he enlisted
in Company G of the Massachusetts Volunteers, leaving his wife and nine
children at home. He was wounded at Petersburg, Virginia, and taken
prisoner at Fort Stedman, Virginia. Later he was exchanged and ended the
war a corporal in July, 1865. His replacement until 1869, when he was
reappointed, was James Chase.

During the next eleven years the large Crowell family occupied the
dwelling. They participated in the social life of West Dennis and celebrated
daughters' weddings (according to the *Yarmouth Register's* reporter). In 1880

the Lighthouse Board decided that the light was not needed because of the new Stage Harbor Lighthouse and sold the property. The Crowells moved back into their old home on Fisk Street in West Dennis.

But in 1881 the government changed its mind and reestablished the lighthouse. Captain Samuel Adams Peak of Hyannis became keeper, the third generation of his family in the service. His grandfather, Samuel, was the first keeper of Point Gammon in 1815. His father, John, served a total of sixty-two years at Point Gammon, Bishop and Clerks, and South Hyannis.

Captain Peak, who had grown up in lighthouses, went to sea as a youth. he became master of the barks *William Robertson* and *Julia F. Carney*, often taking his wife along on voyages to the Mediterranean. On his death in 1906, Russell Eastman became keeper. He served until the light was discontinued in 1914. But history was not through with the Bass River Light.

Sold at auction, the property changed hands twice before Harry K. Noyes of Noyes Buick in Boston bought it for a summer residence. Until 1933 he expanded the main house, built two garages, the Lodge, and a caretaker's house and converted the stable to a guest house. After his death the place was unoccupied for five years.

Then State Senator Everett Stone of Auburn, Massachusetts, bought it in June, 1938. He planned to continue the improvements. But it was too late in the season to start any major projects. So Mrs. Stone advertised for overnight guests to help defray costs. Two local ladies ran the dining room on concession.

Further expansion occurred during the next years, until the 1944 hurricane entirely destroyed the dining room, pushed a number of cottages off their foundations, and covered the grounds with several feet of beach sand.

The Stones rebuilt. Soon even greater expansion was in progress, including two riprap jetties enclosing a small harbor in front of what was now (of course) the Lighthouse Inn. When Everett Stone died in 1947, his son Robert and his wife Mary took over. In 1949, after the Dennis town meeting decided to "go wet" by six votes, the Stones opened their Sand Bar, at the entrance to the property.

Today, Jonathan and Gregory Stone and his wife Pat are the third generation in charge. And the inn can accommodate 140 guests as compared to the twenty-five of 1938. But most significant is the fact that the Bass River Light shines again.

During the summer of 1989 the Stones installed a modern optic in the

Figure 18.2   The Lighthouse Inn. Courtesy of the Stone family.

old tower as a private aid to navigation. After seventy-six years of darkness, a light was again displayed. It was lit on August 7, 1989—the two hundredth anniversary of the Lighthouse Service. Henceforth, from May 1 to October 31, Bass River's white light will flash every six seconds, lighting the way home for the heavy boat traffic in Nantucket Sound and Bass River.

Figure 18.3   Gregory Stone with their privately-owned 250 mm lantern. Photo by Ron Schloerb, *Cape Cod Times*.

CHAPTER 19

Bishop and Clerks Light

Old Light List No. 107 (Obsolete)
41° 34' 25" N, 70° 15' 01" W
Ht. above water: 59 feet
Fresnel 4th-order lens
Built 1858
Range: 13 miles
Flashing white light
Gray granite tower on ledge
Fog bell
Disestablished 1928
Dynamited 1952

*T*wo and a half miles south of Point Gammon (just east of Hyannis harbor) is a dangerous ledge which extends another mile and a half south. The "Bishop" is the large rock at the north end; the "Clerks" are the smaller rocks to the south.

This is all that remains of a five-acre island almost attached to Point Gammon. Sheep were ferried over and pastured there. But by 1791 Captain Paul Pinkham's famous chart showed "Nantucket Shoals," with over three fathoms between the rocks and Point Gammon.

This dangerous reef needed lighting. So Massachusetts ceded to the United States a site for the light, with the usual concurrent jurisdiction and reversion when the light was no longer in use. A spindle day beacon marked

Figure 19.1 Bishop and Clerks Light (note the extent of the rocks, the remains of an island). National Archives photo.

the shoal in 1851, and in 1855 the new lightship LV4, built in the Boston Navy Yard, was placed there. But the winter of 1856 was so bad for shipping that it was withdrawn.

On August 18, 1856, Congress appropriated $20,000 for building a lighthouse on the reef, and soon construction began. This was a difficult job, somewhat like Eddystone. The granite blocks of the foundation and tower had to be cut to a pattern ashore and then ferried out to the site. Stonework was nearly finished by the end of 1857, and the light went into service on October 1, 1858.

The gray granite sixty-five-foot tower stood on a granite base, and a gray-painted wooden bell tower was attached to its west side. The bell was operated by a weighted clockworks and sounded every thirty seconds when needed. The white light flashed from its fourth-order lens every thirty seconds.

Figure 19.2   Postcard closeup of the light. Courtesy of the Peak family.

The first keeper was John Peak, who had succeeded his father at Point Gammon. His assistant was his son, Samuel Adams Peak, who in 1881 moved to Bass River Light. When John died in 1886, his successor was Charles Hinckley of Hyannis, at four and a half feet probably the shortest keeper known. He stayed at the light until 1923, when the light was automated with acetylene gas (like the large buoys of the time).

Changes to the light were few over the years. In 1887 the Lighthouse Board reported: "A red sector was inserted to cover Cross Rip and Tuckernuck Shoals; 150 tons of riprap stones were placed around the tower for protection of its foundation."

In 1923, in addition to the fuel change a smaller fifth-order lens went in, and the red sector and fog bell were removed. The next year the characteristic of the light became flashing white every ten seconds, with a two-second flash. Finally in 1928, the light was discontinued, and the old tower served as a day beacon.

As the years passed the old tower suffered from vandalism and slow deterioration. As a result, the Coast Guard in 1952 decided that it should be destroyed. Dynamite seemed the best solution. So a professional razer, the U. O. MacDonald Company of Boston, bored sixty-eight holes in the base. Sandbags were packed around it so that the tower would collapse straight down. Timing of the blast was kept secret to avoid possible danger to onlookers.

Just before 1:00 P.M. on September 11, 1952, John Parmenter of Brockton pushed down the detonator plunger, and the proud old tower collapsed into a heap on Bishop Rock. A white slatted pyramidal day beacon, thirty feet tall, marks the grave. The area was considered so dangerous that it became heavily buoyed in addition. A red nun buoy is a mile and a half SSE of the daymark, a red lighted gong buoy, flashing red every four seconds, is closer to the daymark, and a green bell buoy, flashing green every four seconds, is off the northeast end of the shoal.

20

Wood End Light

Light List No. 12385
42° 1.3' N, 70° 11.6 W
Ht. above water: 45 feet
5th-order lens; 190 mm optic
Built 1872
Range: 13 miles
Flashing red every 10 seconds
White square tower
Horn: 1 blast ev. 30 seconds
Solar-powered with batteries

Wood End Light is built on some ten acres where two coastal defense forts were built during the Civil War. These forts were promptly named "Fort Useless" and "Fort Ridiculous" by the men of Provincetown. They presumably served their purpose, for no Confederate cruisers molested the harbor. For years afterward they helped the P'towners celebrate the Fourth of July, so the story goes. The lighthouse is located between Race Point and Long Point, directly across from the harbor of Provincetown.

Wood End's history begins with the appropriation by Congress of $15,000 on June 10, 1872. The Lighthouse Board's annual reports says:

This new light station was completed and lighted for the first time on the night of the 20th of November, 1872. The tower is of brick, pyramidal in form, and is painted brown. The focal plane is . . . 45 feet above the sea. The lens is of the fifth order . . . illuminating the entire horizon, and will show a red light flashing every 15 seconds, which can be seen . . . at a distance of eleven nautical miles. The keeper's dwelling is of wood; one and a half stories high; painted cream-color, and is placed northeastward of the tower.

The greatest reason for this light was the frequency of wrecks nearby. Sailing vessels, often helpless before storm winds, were driven ashore. In his *Cape Cod* Thoreau reports a conversation with one survivor, a carpenter from Maine, en route to Boston:

When the storm came on they endeavored to get into Provincetown harbor. "It was dark and misty," said he. "and as we were steering for

Figure 20.1   Wood End Light, ca. 1880. Courtesy of the Thornton Burgess Museum.

Figure 20.2   Wood End, ca. 1890 (note the new fog-signal house being built). Rosenthal photo, courtesy of Cape Cod Photo Supply.

Long Point Light we suddenly saw the land near us—for our compass was out of order . . . and we immediately struck on the bar. . . . The sea washed completely over us. . . . We all got safe to house in Wood End, at midnight, wet to our skins, and half frozen to death."

Even after the light was lit, disasters occurred—over fifty since 1875. The worst year was 1899, when a sloop and two schooners came ashore and broke up under the pounding of the sea.

By the time Wood End Light came into being, the considerable settlement on the point of some two hundred people, with their own schoolhouse and salt works, had left. But there was still some commercial activity, as the Lighthouse Board reported in 1880:

The keeper of this station is much annoyed by the stench and flies coming from the fish-oil works located between this and Long Point Station.

Figure 20.3   Wood End, 1915. U.S. Coast Guard photo.

In 1896 major changes occurred. The government built another keeper's house of wood, a story and a half high, with six rooms, at a cost of $29,000. They also built a storage shed of 990 square feet for $5000 and an oil house for $1500. In 1900 the Board reported that "A revolving machine, for the optical apparatus, made in the lighthouse machine shop at Boston, was installed."

And in 1902 a bell tower and 1000-pound fog bell were added. Finally in 1911 the town built a stone breakwater across the upper end of the harbor, so that at low tide one could cross from the town to the light, instead of trudging around the end of the harbor through miles of sand.

The single most horrible disaster was the collision just a half-mile south of the light between the Navy submarine *S-4* and the Coast Guard cutter *Paulding* on December 17, 1927. The *S-4* was testing equipment as she rose to the surface, and the *Paulding* had not been informed of her presence. The result: the cutter tore a great hole just forward of the submarine's "sail" and

Figure 20.4   Wood End today (note the solar panels to power the light). U.S. Coast Guard photo.

passed completely over her. Thirty-six men died in seconds; six were able to seal a watertight compartment for a slower death.

Twenty-four hours after the collision a diver, in the clumsy gear of the day, was signaling on the sunken hull in Morse code with a hammer:

"Are you alive?"

"Yes, six of us are alive here," came the Morse in reply.

"Everything possible is being done to help you."

"The air is very bad in here. Please hurry."

Frenzied efforts by every available Navy facility in the face of extreme cold were futile. A day later came the last tapped message: "We cannot live beyond six o'clock."

On January 4, 1928, eighteen days after the collision, two huge air-filled pontoons, towed to the scene from Norfolk, Virginia, finally raised the *S-4* to the surface. Perhaps the best wry comment on the event was that of Seaman Walter Bishop. Among his water-soaked effects was a long poem describing the "pigboats," which begins:

> *In the cantankerous mind of the devil*
> *There festered a fiendish scheme,*
> *He called his cohorts together,*
> *And they designed the submarine.*

The lighthouse was manned until 1961, when the dwellings and storage shed were razed and the light was fully automated. A modern aerobeacon replaced the fourth-order Fresnel lens. Instead of installing a generator at the station, an electric pole line was run to the light. Then in 1979 four acres, including the station and the life-saving station at Herring Cove Beach, were turned over to the Navy. Solar panels mounted on the south side of the tower in 1981, with batteries in the tower, now provide power for the light.

Today Wood End is a lonely, unattended tower, still showing its red danger signal out to the horizon eleven miles away. It warns the busy fishing fleet and recreational boaters to give it a wide berth if they want to clear the point and enter the snug little harbor of Provincetown.

Stage Harbor Light

Light List No. 12995
41° 39.5' N, 69° 59.1' W
Ht. above water: 41 feet
Fresnel 5th-order lens
Built 1880
Range: 12 miles
Fixed white light
White tower, walkway to house
Disestablished 1933, replaced by modular tower, flashing
  white every six seconds, range 8 miles
Privately owned today

*A*lmost three hundred years before 1880, the snug harbor that became Stage Harbor in Chatham entered history. In the fall of 1606 Champlain's second expedition got into trouble on the Monomoy shoals, lost a rudder, and put in for repairs. Dr. Henry Kittredge describes what happened next:

> *After [the stay] had gone on for a fortnight, the Indians began to wonder what the end would be; . . . so they decided to speed their guests into departure. . . . Early in the morning the Indians crept up on the shore party, found all but one asleep, and let fly four hundred arrows, such a volley that "to rise up was death." The*

**Figure 21.1   Stage Harbor Light (note the harbor channel
just beyond the light). National Archive photo.**

*Frenchmen fled. . . ; the Indians meanwhile making a "desperate
noise with roaring which it was terrible to hear."*

The name "Stage Harbor" goes back to the date (June 11, 1712) of
Chatham's incorporation as a town. The lighthouse is also known as
Harding's Beach Light. In the 1876 report of the Lighthouse Board was this
recommendation:

*The establishment of a light at this place, giving a good range with
one of the Chatham lights, would serve as a guide into Old Stage
Harbor, and would be of great value to vessels seeking refuge there
at night and during bad weather.*

And Chatham is one of the foggiest places on the East Coast.

As a result, Congress on March 3, 1879, appropriated $10,000 "for a light
at Stage Harbor in the State of Massachusetts." Then, on May 24, 1879, the
town's Proprietors of Common Lands named a committee:

Figure 21.2   Stage Harbor in the 1890's. Courtesy of George K. Harding.

This Committee is to deal with Mr Tower the Government Agent in regards to the price made by the Proprietors . . . two hundred and fifty dollars for the Ground to Build a new Lite House they are instructed to use their Best Judgment in regards the price & Location for the Lite House.

Payment for the three acres was finally made on December 4, 1879.

During 1880 an iron tower (of the same design as Chatham's latest pair) and a frame keeper's dwelling were built at a cost of $9,882.74. Into the lantern went a fifth-order lens with a range of twelve miles. The four-wick lamp was first lit on July 15, 1990, showing a fixed white light all around the horizon.

Perched on the edge of the channel into Stage Harbor, the lighthouse marked the entrance for the lively fishing and commercial traffic of the time. Even "Old Ironsides" visited there, according to the log of talkative Josiah Hardy of Chatham. She would long since have been scrapped had it not been for Dr. Oliver Wendell Holmes of Boston, who in 1830 (aged twenty-one) wrote his famous plea for her life that begins:

Ay, tear her tattered ensign down!
Long has it waved on high,
And many an eye has danced to see
That banner in the sky.

The poem was a rousing success. Schoolchildren of that generation donated their pennies to help save the ship, and for generations after 1830 they learned the poem by heart. One of our most treasured symbols, she is today a familiar sight in Boston harbor.

A series of keepers inhabited the comfortable, clapboarded house, beginning with Enoch Eldredge, who received a salary of $560 a year until his death on March 7, 1884. Next came Charles Ireland, who resigned in 1904. He was followed by Joseph Wood, who stayed only two years before transferring to another station.

The next keeper, Alfred A. Howard, achieved a fine reputation for saving lives. He received several commendations. For example, Walter C. Harding capsized in his dory but managed to cling to the bottom. Keeper Howard saw the accident and went to the rescue, and, in Harding's words:

Had it not been for the prompt assistance of A.A. Howard . . . it would have ended seriously. . . . I was taken from the bottom of my dory and carried to the lighthouse where I was furnished with dry clothing and made as comfortable as possible.

On December 14, 1914, Captain Ephraim Smith of West Chatham wrote the inspector in Boston that Keeper Howard had saved his horse from drowning. The horse and wagon had become mired in quicksand and the driver called for help. Howard responded and skillfully rescued the animal before the tide came in. Captain Smith wrote: "And as he would not take money for his very kind service, I take these means to write you for your kind consideration towards commending him."

Howard received his commendation from Secretary of Commerce Redfield. That year he was also one of seven keepers in the district to receive an efficiency star, and the next year he received a $40 raise to $600 per year. He transferred to another station in 1916.

His successor was Mills Gunderson, transferred from Boston Light and receiving the same salary. He earned an efficiency star in 1918. The old house, with its "gingerbread" along the eaves, saw tragedy at least once: Captain Gunderson hanged himself in the shed out back on June 15, 1919. Nobody ever knew why—or, as an informant said, "They ain't sayin'."

His son, Stanley Gunderson, who had been discharged from the Army in 1918, followed his father, receiving a salary of $780 a year to start. He served until June 30, 1933, when the light was decommissioned. During those fourteen years his salary rose gradually to $1380 per year, and beginning in 1920 he received commendations for the excellent condition of his station.

He too performed several rescues. One was of the yacht *Golliway*, which ran aground about a quarter-mile SSW of the station on October 12, 1929. He reported:

> *. . . as it was very near high water I proceeded at once to their assistance with my own powerboat, as if I had of attempted to summon other and the tide would have been ebbed too far to attempt to pull them off. With my boat I succeeded in pulling the bow around to deep water; . . . So I ran anchors offshore. . . , then took the occupants of the yacht to my station and furnished them with food and dry clothing as soon as I got them ashore.*

Next morning the Coast Guard, alerted by Gunderson, pulled the yacht free and into Stage Harbor. For this action Commissioner George Putnam of the Lighthouse Service officially commended Gunderson for "his timely assistance in this instance."

Even the passageway to the light had its share of history, so the story goes. During Prohibition days, when the Cape was awash with more than water, the floorboards often concealed large caches of liquor. During one surprise inspection, allegedly, the inspector walked across the hiding place while the keeper sweated for a moment. But he was merely told to nail down those loose floor-boards.

The days of Stage Harbor Light were numbered. On June 16, 1933, it was replaced by an unwatched light on a skeleton tower 308 feet SSW of the tower. Stanley Gunderson complained bitterly to the press that this step was hardly economical or wise:

> *The present light is easily visible 18 miles [really twelve] yet the lighthouse bureau decides [in favor of] an unattended light of 260 candlepower (replacing 680 c. p.) supposed to show 10 miles, but which after a storm or two which crusts the lens with salt, will easily show 3 or 4 miles at the most on a good clear night.*

But his ironic comment, and his argument that such a step would be more expensive, did no good, and he was out of a job. He remained in the service,

**Figure 21.3   The light today. The lantern has been removed
and the property is privately owned. Courtesy of George K.
Harding.**

however, and on March 26, 1934, he became assistant keeper at Great Point
Light on Nantucket at a salary of $1320. A year later he resigned from the
service.

Several years later the property was declared surplus, and the Hoyt
family bought it, after the lantern had been removed and the tower capped.
For many years they used the lively Victorian house as a summer home.
Weddings and honeymoons occurred there, as shown in the daily log kept by
the family. The property is still owned by the Hoyts.

Today, looking out of the kitchen window from the keeper's house of
this last lighthouse built on Cape Cod, one can still see a variety of traffic
passing close by: stately yawls and schooners with their brass gleaming,
humble scallopers heading for the rich beds just offshore, sport fishermen
with their outriggers swaying, even the ever-present Sailfish and board
sailors. And the light, on its modular tower, flashes white every six seconds,
with a range of eight miles.

22

Early Nantucket

*N*antucket, like Cape Cod and Martha's Vineyard, is the product of glacial action during the Ice Ages. It is surrounded by dangerous shoals—and hence an ideal place for lighthouses. This the inhabitants quickly realized; they built their own town-funded Brant Point Light in 1746, only thirty years after our very first lighthouse—Boston's.

Europeans first saw Nantucket when the Cabots explored our coasts in 1497 and 1498. In 1602 Bartholomew Gosnold explored the sound, named Cape Cod and other places, and undoubtedly sighted the island.

The next mention is in a grant by King James I to the Earl of Stirling of "Pemaquid and its Dependencies . . . together with Long Island and the adjacent Islands." The earl, in 1641, sold "for forty pounds to Thomas Mayhew, a Merchant of Watertown, in Massachusetts, and Thomas Mayhew, his son, the Island of Nantucket, with several small Islands adjacent [Martha's Vineyard and the Elizabeth Islands]."

That same year (1641) Mayhew sold most of his interest in Nantucket to ten men led by Tristram Coffin for thirty pounds "and also two bever hats one for myself and one for my wife." In 1664 the ten proprietors bought from Wanackmamack and Nicanoose, the two chief sachems, most of their land. Later there was much trouble over land titles because the Indians did not understand that selling their land meant they could no longer use it.

Settlement of the island had several reasons. First, perhaps, was economic opportunity. Second was escape from the religious absolutism of the Massachusetts Bay colony. For example, by 1658 Quakers were banished under pain of death, and two Quakers were hanged in Boston in 1659.

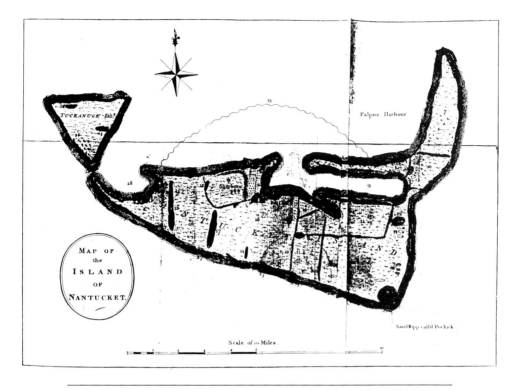

Figure 22.1   Early map of Nantucket. From Crevecoeur,
***Letters from an American Farmer*, 1784.**

The first settlers, in 1659, were Thomas Macy and his wife and five children (only one of whom survived), Edward Starbuck, and Isaac Coleman. With the help of the natives, they survived that first winter, for game was plentiful and there was plenty of Indian corn.

That spring Edward Starbuck reported to the proprietors, and soon Tristram Coffin and the others came and chose their home lots, each of which "shall contain sixty rods square to a whole share [22½ acres]." By 1720 most families were in or near present-day Nantucket town. Many of the original names still exist there: Coffin, Starbuck, Swain, Folger, Gardner, Coleman.

At first farming, sheep and cattle raising, fishing, and hunting concerned the new community. Soon a grist mill was needed, and Peter Folger became miller, as well as surveyor, blacksmith, weaver, town clerk, and interpreter. In due course he also became Benjamin Franklin's grandfather.

The town was incorporated in 1641 and named Sherburne by the New

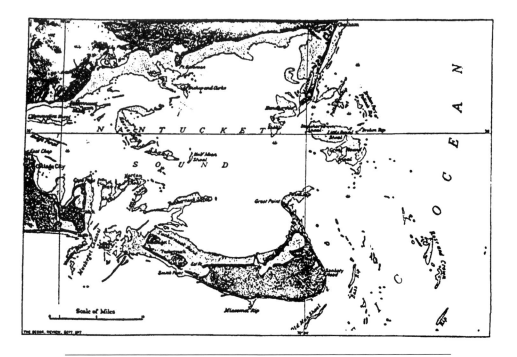

**Figure 22.2   Nantucket Sound, showing the principal
shoals. From Starbuck, *History of Nantucket*.**

York governor, who claimed jurisdiction by a 1664 grant to the Duke of York
from King Charles II. Much confusion and dissension resulted from that grant,
until finally the islands became Massachusetts counties.

But the soil of the island was thin and poor, and soon Nantucketers took
to the sea for a living. Whaling became a mainstay of the economy, first small
boats offshore, and then bigger and bigger ships roaming the world's oceans
for whale oil. Thomas Jefferson reported that from 1771–1775 150 of the 303
Massachusetts whaling ships were from Nantucket.

With the Revolution, this rich state of affairs crumbled, thanks to
England's policies, and the Massachusetts legislature, fearing that the island
would help the British, threatened a complete embargo. This would have
meant starvation. The Sherburne selectmen made an impassioned appeal,
pointing out that the island could not defend itself and was not supplying
British fisheries. The General Court repealed the embargo.

The situation was desperate. Pacifist Quakers were strong and there was
a large loyalist group. During the war years, the British captured over one

hundred ships, mostly whalers, and by 1779 all local sources of firewood were depleted.

Somehow Nantucket weathered the Revolution, and slowly the whaling industry revived. In 1811 twenty-four whalers set forth. But then came the War of 1812, and British cruisers were so numerous that waterborne supplies ran far short of need.

For example, corn, when available, sold for $1.25 a bushel and flour for $13.50 a barrel. Obed Macy describes the situation:

Such a picture of distress had not been displayed since the Revolutionary War. Previous to the war, not a beggar was to be seen in the streets; at this time many received their daily pittance from the hand of charity.

When the war ended, whaling revived rapidly; by 1819 sixty-one vessels were in the trade. But this was the beginning of the end. Twenty towns and cities as far away as New York were also whaling, cutting into Nantucket's lion's share.

The census of 1820 shows how the population had grown since the seven first settlers of 1659, and the age breakdown is interesting. Under ten, males and females were in equal numbers: 875 to 861. But over forty-five, women outnumbered men by over 50%: 757 to 484. There were 274 colored persons, and total population was 7,266. Indians were not counted. A plague in 1763–1764 killed two-thirds of the 358 then alive, leaving a mere 136. A century earlier there had been 1500.

Brant Point Light

Light List No. 13915
41° 17.4' N, 70° 05.5' W
Ht. above water: 26 feet
Various lamps; 4th-order lens (1856); 250 mm lantern
First built 1746; rebuilt 9 times (last in 1901)
Range: 10 miles
Occulting red every four seconds
White tower with footbridge
Radio beacon: 325 kHz, BP
Horn: 1 blast every 10 seconds

*B*rant Point Light, guiding ships into Nantucket harbor, holds several lighthouse records: (1) it is the second oldest lighthouse (after Boston); (2) it is the most often rebuilt lighthouse on this coast; (3) the present lighthouse is the shortest in operation today.

Its reason for existence was, quite simply, the preeminence of Nantucket in the whaling industry. A large fleet of whalers brought in the whale oil and smaller ships exported it to the other colonies and to Europe. A light for the harbor was a practical necessity.

So the independent Nantucketers at a town meeting on January 24, 1746, voted two hundred pounds and chose three men "to take care to build the lighthouse . . . on Brant Point." The town expressed the hope that "the owners of, or others concerned in, shipping will maintain the light therein."

But apparently, with no set fee system, the town actually maintained the light until 1758, when it burned to the ground.

Soon, in 1759, another lighthouse was built. These first lights were simple lanterns hoisted onto platforms, very fire-prone. This second light lasted until 1774, when, said the *Massachusetts Gazette*:

> *... On Wednesday the 9th of March Instant ... they had a most violent gust of Wind that perhaps was ever known there but it lasted only about a Minute. . . . It seemed to come in a narrow Vein, and in its progress blew down and totally destroyed the Light-House on that Island, besides several Shops, Barns, etc.*

Clearly this was a tornado, as we would call it today.

Now that the town could charge fees to maintain the light, as approved by the legislature in 1774, a third structure was quickly built, and it lasted until 1783, when it too burned. That year the fourth lighthouse, which had a wooden lantern with glass windows, hoisted between two spars, went into service. But it gave such a weak light that soon seamen began calling it a "bug light," comparing it to the flash of a lightning bug. This light burned in 1786, and the fifth lighthouse—no real improvement—was destroyed in a storm in 1788.

The town soon built a sixth lighthouse. It was this one that Massachusetts ceded to the United States in 1795. And that same year the town changed its name from Sherburne to Nantucket. This light lasted until 1825, when it was condemned.

Reliability was sometimes a problem. Take the case of the whaler *William Penn*, stranded on a reef near Brant Point in 1817. The *Nantucket Gazette* reported on January 17:

> *The brig* William Penn *struck on a shoal. . . . On Wednesday morning at 3 o'clock three of her owners proceeded to Brant Point to get her off—when every lamp in the lighthouse was out. They proceeded to the lamp-lighter's house and awoke him. . . . This may serve as a caution to Mariners how they place dependence on the lights on their present system.*

In 1824 Congress appropriated $1600 for a seventh light and keeper's dwelling. Obed Macy did not think much of the design, for he wrote in his diary:

A strangely constructed lighthouse is now erected on Brant Point. On a 20 ft. roof above there is to be placed the lamps; which is to be supported by stout pieces of timber . . . Instead of this there ought to be a high stone lighthouse placed at the end of the point.

The lantern contained eight lamps, each with its reflector.

The channels over Nantucket bar were constantly shifting. So as early as 1762 the town had voted for a "Beacon in some Convenient Place as a mark for Vessels to come in at the East Channel." Lining up the lighthouse and the beacon led ships right down the channel and into the harbor. In 1820 the Lighthouse Establishment built a permanent beacon consisting of a single lamp with a large reflector atop a small keeper's hut. Caleb Cushman became the first keeper of the beacon at $150 a year. As the channel shifted, this range light had to be rebuilt and moved in 1856, 1861, and 1869. It was discontinued in 1881. Today there is a range beacon.

Finally the need for a permanent, solid structure was seen, and in 1854 Congress appropriated $15,000 "for rebuilding the lighthouse at Brant's Point, Nantucket." The entire amount—to the penny—was spent in 1856 and 1857

Figure 23.1   The tenth Brant Point Light, with the eighth tower in the background. Courtesy of William P. Quinn.

**Figure 23.2 Brant Point today, as seen from the water.
Photo by Dr. Richard Sommers, 1990.**

to build a brick tower attached to a new keeper's house. The *Nantucket Mirror* described the tower on November 22, 1856:

> *The foundation of the tower is of concrete cement, two feet thick, and eighteen feet in diameter. . . . The base of the tower is of hammered granite, laid in courses two feet thick, to the height of twelve feet. . . . A circular iron stairway winds its spiral way up to a floor of iron, where rests the lantern, 58 feet above the foundation and 47 feet above the ground.*

The new keeper's house was as solidly built, on a granite foundation, thirty-two feet by twenty-eight feet, of brick, two stories high, on the same level as the light. The bricks were laid in the best of cement "so as to prevent dampness," according to the builders. But the house has always been very damp; one observer in 1907 noted that the inside walls were covered with moisture.

Figure 23.3   Airview of both Brant Point Lights. U.S. Coast Guard photo.

On December 10, 1856, this eighth Brant Point lighthouse was lit. In the lantern was a fourth-order Fresnel lens (or "catadioptric apparatus," as it was called), showing a fixed red light.

Land quarrels play a large part in the history of Brant Point. Because of some confusion, early in the 1800's the Proprietors of Common and Undivided Lands granted several house lots on government land. Then, when the Lighthouse Board began fencing in its property, residents sued. The case dragged on for many years. Finally the Lighthouse Board settled the matter by selling the five house lots containing three summer homes and part of a hotel.

The harbor channel kept shifting, building sand up in front of the light. So in 1900 it was necessary to install a fixed red beacon some six hundred feet nearer the harbor entrance. Then in 1901 the present (and tenth) Brant Point lighthouse, a short wooden tower, was built. It was lit on January 31, 1901. At first it showed the same fixed red light, but now the current *Light List* lists it as occulting red every four seconds, twenty-six feet above water, visible ten miles.

Changes since 1901 have been few. In 1908 two new range towers were built, lining up the wide dredged channel. In the 1930's a seawall and boathouse were built, and in the 1950's two buildings of the Life-Saving Service were moved to the site to become the Coast Guard station. The fog-bell tower was removed, and the candlepower of the light gradually increased to 13,000 in 1981.

Records of early keepers' names are sketchy until the Lighthouse Board began in 1852 to keep lists of keepers, so that we know that since 1853 there have been fifteen keepers at the station; one of them, Mary Chapman, was the widow of John Chapman. The longest tour was Richard Dixon's (1911–1927), after which he was transferred to Beverly. And the last civilian keeper was Gerald Reed, who served from 1926 until the Coast Guard took over in 1939.

Great Point Light

Light List No. 530
41° 23.4' N, 70° 02.9 W
Ht. above water: 158 feet
14 lamps; Fresnel lens (1857); 190 mm lantern (1986)
Built 1785; rebuilt 1818 and 1986
Range: 14 miles
Flashing white every 5 seconds with red sector 084°–106°
White tower

*T*he history of Great Point (originally called Sandy Point) Light begins at a town meeting on January 10, 1770. They voted to ask the General Court "to build a lighthouse on the end of Sandy Point." This is the northeastern, sandy tip of the island.

Time passed (including the Revolution), and on February 5, 1784, the legislature approved building the light. In November they voted 1389 pounds "for the erecting of a lighthouse and small house on Nantucket." Quickly the lighthouse rose. On June 10, 1790, Massachusetts ceded the property to the United States.

Captain Paul Pinkham was the first keeper—a fine choice. He had gone whaling and in the coastal trade. But his greatest contribution to local navigation was "A Chart of Nantucket Shoals Surveyed by Captain Paul Pinkham." It made him famous. Published in Boston in 1791, it showed all the shoals of Nantucket and Vineyard Sounds.

**Figure 24.1   Second Great Point Light (note the ground lead
from the lightning rod). U.S. Coast Guard photo.**

His bills for oil (only the best spermaceti) cost thirty-six pounds per ton of about 1800 gallons. From May 1793 to May 1794 the lighthouse used some 1600 gallons. His salary was $250 per year, which was raised after an eloquent appeal. For example, the twelve cords of wood allowed him cost $96—almost half his pay. He died in 1799 and was succeeded by George Swain.

The next keeper that we know of was Jonathan Coffin in 1812. Since there was no housing at the station, he had to walk the seven miles from town to trim the lamps. His appeal for "hardship pay" was granted by Albert Gallatin, then Secretary of the Treasury, who began to plan for a house near the light, and eventually it was built.

But then in November, 1816, this first wooden lighthouse burned to the ground (some, without proof, suspected arson). Captain Winslow Lewis's *Description of the Light Houses* of 1817 updates the situation, describing the temporary light on a triangle thirty-six feet high, visible three or four leagues (nine to twelve miles) in clear weather.

Nantucket (Great Point) Light Station Mass
SE   ½ mile   *L. H. List 1892.*

Figure 24.2   Great Point Light from the sea. From *Light House List, 1892.*

On March 3, 1817, Congress appropriated $7500 to rebuild, and the classically shaped stone tower familiar to generations of Nantucketers was completed in 1818 at a cost of $7,385.12. Then in 1825 Congress finally voted $1600 for a keeper's house, providing accommodations at the light for the keeper's family.

Edward Carpender inspected the station in 1838; his report said:

Seven miles from Nantucket harbor . . . stands the great light of Nantucket. This light is 70 feet above the sea. . . . It consists of 14 lamps, 3 with fifteen and 11 with sixteen-inch reflectors, arranged in the usual way. . . . This being an exterior and important light, I propose no reduction of it. Premises in sufficient order.

1857 was an important year for the Nantucket lighthouses. Both Brant Point and Great Point received Fresnel lenses. At the same time Great Point received an assistant keeper's house and the tower was lined with brick.

During the years between 1863 and 1890, forty-three vessels were wrecked near Great Point. Apparently confusion between that light and the Cross Rip lightship was sometimes to blame; they both were fixed lights. On April 17, 1864, for instance, three vessels went ashore on Great Point Rip. Then a schooner smashed to bits on the bar in October, 1865. The captain, his wife and children, and the crew were able to row to the station. And there were three wrecks in 1866 nearby.

So the toll of ships went—and nothing was done to correct the problem until 1889, when a red sector in the light marked Cross Rip and the other shoals south of it. This action reduced the wrecks, but as late as 1915 the *Marcus L. Urann* stranded on Wasque Shoal, and the keeper aided in the rescue of "13 men, one woman, and a cat." For his efforts he received the Life Saving Medal.

During the 1880's several events of note occurred. In 1882 mineral oil (kerosene) supplanted lard oil in the lamp, and in 1889 the double dwelling was condemned as too small for two families and demolished. In its place rose a larger framed double house, thirty-seven by twenty-seven feet with a large ell, on the same foundation.

In the Washington archives are many logs from Great Point. Here are some excerpts, with the weather details omitted:

1910   *Sept 22—*   *Azalea [lighthouse tender] landed 10 tons coal 2 cords wood and and annual supplies & 450 gallons of oil. Hibiscus [tender] landed 250 gallons oil.*

   Sept 26—   *Busy carting up some of the oil today*

   Sept 27—   "   "   "   "   "

   Sept 30—   *Finished carting up oil today*

   Oct. 25—   *Hibiscus landed potatoes and onions 2.30 pm.*

   Dec. 18—   *Three masted schooner ashore in the chord of the bay.*

   Dec. 19—   *Revenue cutter's Mohawk and Acushnet made attempt to pull off schooner but failed.*

   Dec. 29—   *Schooner Garland floated @ 8:30*

The keeper's duties included some truly back-breaking labor. All of these supplies had to be hauled up from the beach and stowed.

The "great light of Nantucket," as Edward Carpender called it, stood firm, but on February 16, 1968, a suspicious fire leveled the keepers' dwelling. Then on March 29, 1984, a monster storm totally destroyed the old stone tower.

The islanders, with the help of Senator Kennedy, persuaded Congress to

Figure 24.3   The trawler *Calypso* lost power and came ashore on November 30, 1990. The tug *Jaguar* pulled her off twelve hours later. Airview by Steve Heaslip, *Cape Cod Times*.

vote the funds to rebuild at a cost almost two hundred times the 1818 price of $7,365.12. A replica of the original was built, with a core of reinforced concrete five feet thick at the bottom. It has a veneer of rubble stones from the old tower. The only visible difference is an extra window for solar cells (with batteries in the tower) to power the 9,283 candlepower light. It has the same red sector as before and flashes white every five seconds, with a range of fourteen miles.

On September 6, 1986, as the new light was turned on, Senator Kennedy christened the tower with a bottle of champagne. With him was Alice Berry, granddaughter of Judah Berry, keeper in 1900.

**Figure 24.4   The March, 1984 storm leveled the 1818 tower.
Courtesy of *Cape Cod Times*.**

**Figure 24.5   The replica tower, lit on September 8, 1986
(note the solar panel). Courtesy of William P. Quinn.**

Sankaty Head Light

Light List No. 540
41° 17' N, 70° 02.9' W
Ht. above water: 158 feet
4th-order Fresnel lens (1849); aerobeacons (1950)
Built 1849
Range: 24 miles
Flashing white every 7.5 seconds
White tower with red band in the middle

*S*ankaty Head is a commanding bluff some ninety feet above the sea on the east coast of Nantucket. With such height, very early the inshore whalers set up a whale-watching post there. It also commands a view of shoals such as the Rose and Crown, the Old Man, Great Rip, Bass Rip, and others. These are truly dangerous waters.

In 1838 "A Sailor" expressed in the *Boston Post* a common feeling among seamen of the time:

Now, the difficulty to us is that we have no directions to govern us in going through the passage, except some vague ones in Blunt's Coastal Pilot. None of these directions would answer for the night time. What the mariner wants is . . . a lighthouse on Sankaty Head. . . . [It] would mark a place of refuge for any ship running into a strong westerly.

Figure 25.1   An early drawing of Sankaty Head Light.

Demand for a light grew stronger and stronger. On August 14, 1848, Congress appropriated $18,000 (later $2000 more) for a light, keeper's dwelling, and purchase of a second-order (almost the largest) lens from Lapaute in Paris. The Fifth Auditor reported on December 29, 1849, that "This lighthouse has just been finished in a superior manner . . . at an expense of $10,333 [not counting the cost of the lens]." George Myrick had sold the government ten acres on May 29, 1849, for $250.

All of the materials came into Nantucket harbor (halfway across the island) and were carted to the cliff. Quickly the sixty-foot tower and brick keeper's house were built and the lens installed. The clockworks (run by heavy weights hanging down the inside of the tower) were in use until 1933, when the light was electrified and a motor was installed to turn the lens. The lantern's windows were of half-inch plate glass to protect the lens from fascinated birds and violent storms. The *Nantucket Inquirer* reported on February 4, 1850 that:

> *The new lighthouse at Sankaty Head was lighted for the first time on Friday evening [February 1]. The flashes of light are very brilliant and must be visible at a distance of twenty-five miles.*

Finally the Lighthouse Service was catching up with technology. Sankaty was a fixed white light varied with flashes every one and one-half minutes

**Figure 25.2   The light painted brown. Courtesy of the
Nantucket Historical Association.**

(FVF is the lighthouse code). Later it showed a brilliant ten-second flash with
a fixed white fifty-second light.

The first report of the new Lighthouse Board (January 30, 1852) includes
a two-page discussion of the lighthouse, saying:

> *The present keeper [Captain Alexander D. Bunker, a veteran
> shipmaster] took charge of the light on the night it was first lighted,
> without previous knowledge or instruction as to its management,
> but encountered no other difficulty than that arising from the use of
> bad oil.*

Sankaty became a popular place to visit during the summer, and the
lighthouse was adapted accordingly. The *Nantucket Mirror* remarked on
October 25, 1856, that:

> *The narrow aperture in the platform under the lantern . . . has been
> widened to allow ladies with hoop skirts to pass up through to see the
> reflectors.*

Figure 25.3 Keeper Joseph Remsen and his family. Courtesy of the Nantucket Historical Association.

In 1875 Samuel Adams Drake visited the lighthouse and wrote that: "Fishermen call it the blazing star. Its flashes are very full, vivid, and striking, and its position is of great importance, as warning the mariner to steer wide of the great South Shoal."

In that same year a newly developed wick, called an "English wick," was adopted. According to the keeper's log of November 19, 1875, it required trimming only once a night instead of the three or four of the former wicks. This the keepers welcomed; it made their lives easier.

After the Civil War many keepers were veterans. Uriah Clark served until 1873, when he died and was succeeded by George Folger. Charles Swain, Franklin Murphy, Freeman Atkins, Benjamin Sayer, and Charles Pollard served short terms as assistants.

The 1880's saw a number of changes. In 1886 the U.S. Signal Corps ran a telegraph and telephone line to the lighthouse. In addition a fifty-foot flagpole was installed to display storm signals. And in 1887 the brick keeper's house was razed, and a wooden double house was built to accommodate the keeper and his assistant, who until then had had to live off the station.

A major improvement occurred in 1888. A crew came down from Boston (with their own cook!) and removed the badly corroded deck and lantern, raised the tower ten feet, and renewed deck and lantern. Now the light could reach even farther. While the work was being done, a fixed light shone from a temporary tower until November, 1888.

During all these years, even with the great light, a great many vessels have run afoul of the shoals off Sankaty. Perhaps the earliest recorded was the Dutch ship *Exportation*, in 1673. The cargo and crew were saved, but the ship was destroyed. In 1774 in fine weather two whalers came to grief on Great Rip; luckily the crews survived. The list goes on and on.

After several ocean voyages and a stint in the Life-Saving Service, Joseph Remsen became keeper in 1892 and served until 1919. He had seven assistants, all of whom later became head keepers. Two of them, Charles Vanderhoop (a Gay Head Indian) and Eugene Larsen, served at Sankaty. Larsen served thirty-nine years there, receiving several Superintendent's Pennants for excellence.

Sankaty Light was electrified in 1933, increasing the candlepower to 720,000, and in 1938 the century-old clockworks gave way to a small electric motor. Then in 1950 the classic lens was removed from the lantern, to be replaced by two aerobeacons. Its final resting place is the Nantucket Whaling Museum.

In 1970 the Coast Guard removed the lantern and deck and replaced it with an "odd-shaped aluminum cap," as the Nantucketers called it. This caused the light to sweep over nearby houses and blind motorists. A flood of protests caused the Coast Guard to reconsider and put back the deck and lantern, so that Sankaty again "looked like a lighthouse."

Today Sankaty Head, with the light 158 feet above the sea, flashes every seven and a half seconds, with a range of twenty-four miles. Unfortunately about 1939 the Coast Guard razed the fine old double keepers' dwelling of 1888 and replaced it with ranch-style housing for its keepers.

**Figure 25.4   Sankaty Head in January, 1992. Note closeness
of cliff edge. Photo by Steve Heaslip, *Cape Cod Times*.**

Early Martha's Vineyard

Martha's Vineyard, lying west of Nantucket, was also sighted by the early explorers. Some historians say that Gosnold landed there and planted corn and wheat. The island was included in the grant by the Earl of Stirling to Thomas Mayhew and his son in 1641, and it became their home. Because of the character of Mayhew and the conditions of a later grant, the Vineyard suffered long years of nearly absolute rule.

At some time during 1642 Mayhew visited his domain and chose his home lot. Soon afterward he granted five men (later twenty) authority equal to his (which he then ignored) to permit further colonists. Only one of the five—John Daggett—actually settled there.

When the first settlement began is still unclear. But Thomas's great-grandson Experience writes:

> *In 1642 he [Thomas Mayhew] sends Mr. Thomas Mayhew Junior his only Son, . . . with some other Persons . . . where they settled at the East End, and quickly after the Father followed.*

For ten years the colony clung to a meager existence: about three dozen settlers among 3000 Indians, who wanted nothing to do with the whites. They remembered previous poor treatment: Champlain's battle in 1606, and kidnappings in 1614. But the peaceful attitudes of the settlers eventually turned suspicion into acceptance.

The 1664 grant to the Duke of York (see "Nantucket") caused confusion on the island. In 1669 the governor of New York invited Mayhew to come and

Figure 26.1   The Earl of Stirling, who sold the island to Thomas Mayhew. From Banks, *History of Martha's Vineyard.*

sort out the claims. Two years later Matthew Mayhew made the voyage, and on July 7, 1671, Thomas Mayhew was named governor for life:

> *It is ordered and agreed upon that the said Mr. Thomas Mayhew shall dureing his naturall life bee Governor of the Island. . . , both over the English Inhabitants and the Indians, for the wch bee shall have a commission.*

Mayhew, then eighty, became in effect Lord of the Manor of Tisbury and Chief Justice of both Nantucket and the Vineyard, as well as Governor for life. The price was "to bee 6 Barrells of Fish." Of course, this act violated the original patent's terms and caused great dissension as the Mayhews clung grimly to what they saw as their rights.

The twenty original leaders appealed to Massachusetts for help, but they were rebuffed. As a result Governor Mayhew punished the rebels by confiscatory fines and arrest. Many of the twenty were driven off the island because they wanted political freedom.

Finally the old governor died on March 25, 1682, at eighty-five, and the political climate changed. A new charter from William and Mary, dated October 7, 1691, gave Massachusetts jurisdiction over "the Isles of Capawick [the Indian name for the Vineyard] and Nantuckett near Cape Cod."

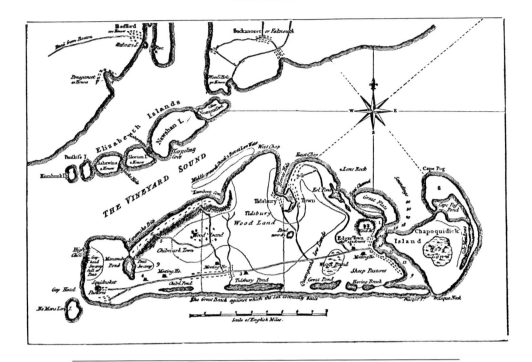

Figure 26.2   Early map of Martha's Vineyard. From Crevecoeur, *Letters from an American Farmer*, 1784.

Suddenly in 1723 New York sent a demand for the yearly six barrels of fish due since the charter of 1671. Disturbed, the islanders appealed to Massachusetts and were told to ignore the demand. Nothing happened.

But not all Mayhews followed the path of old Thomas. His son became a minister and set about converting the Indians. A contemporary tells of his work:

> *With great Compassion he beheld the wretched* Natives . . . *perishing in utter Ignorance of the* true GOD . . . , *laboring under strange Delusions, Inchantments, and panick Fears of* Devils.

He learned the Wampanoag language and translated parts of the Bible, and by 1651 he reported that he had converted "an hundred and ninetie nine men women and children." In 1657 he set sail for England to enlist support for his work and was lost at sea.

His father took over the work, and by 1670 had established an Indian church. In 1682 John Mayhew, son of Thomas, Junior, succeeded his grandfather but died in 1688. His son Experience became the fourth Mayhew to serve the church. In 1709 he published the *Psalms of David* in Wampanoag, and he

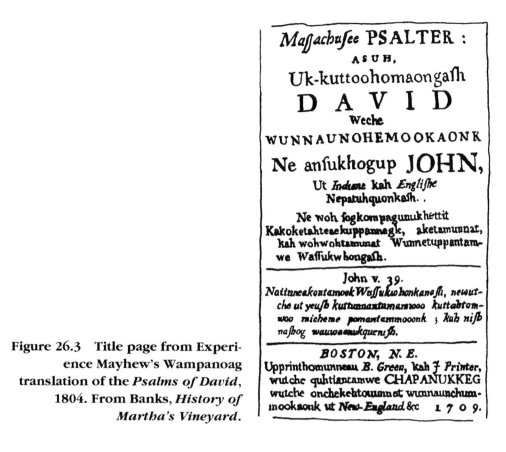

Figure 26.3 Title page from Experience Mayhew's Wampanoag translation of the *Psalms of David*, 1804. From Banks, *History of Martha's Vineyard*.

served sixty-four years, until 1758. His son Zachariah succeeded him for another thirty-nine years. The Mayhew ministry ended in 1806, after 162 years.

While the Revolution was brewing, Massachusetts had three companies of troops on the island, but in 1776 the General Court withdrew them, leaving the island undefended. Like Nantucket, the island suffered from the British blockade, but they were also invaded.

On September 9, 1778, General Sir Charles Grey, with 4,333 men and thirty-two ships, arrived after forays at Newport and New Bedford. One of his officers, Major André, tells the story in his journal:

> *He consented not to march into the country provided the inhabitants should immediately furnish 10,000 sheep and 300 oxen with hay for them. Twenty vessels from Rhode Island arrived to take in stock."*

By the fourteenth, 10,574 sheep and 315 cattle had been driven in, with fifty-two tons of hay. The people were told that they could "apply at New York [in British hands] for payment for the Stock." In addition the force destroyed six

**Figure 26.4   Whalers at Edgartown wharf, 1840. From
Banks, *History of Martha's Vineyard*.**

ships, twenty-three whaleboats, and a salt-works. On September 15 the
flotilla left.

Martha's Vineyard also went a-whaling. As early as 1653 there is a record
of cutting up "drift whales." By 1775 the yearly value of the catch was about
$150,000. But the British destroyed the industry in the Revolution. They
would give crews the choice of whaling for them or fighting against their
country. In 1779 there were seventeen British whalers off Brazil, and "all the
officers and men are Americans."

Going to sea was a dangerous business. Two ministers recorded deaths
in Edgartown between 1767 and 1827—130, of whom seventy-two were
listed as "lost at sea," "killed by a whale," and in one case "eaten up by an
alligator in Batavia harbor." Graveyards on the island record many of these
tragedies. One particularly poignant stone in Vineyard Haven reads:

> *John and Lydia*
> > *That lovely pair*
> *A whale killed him*
> > *Her body lies here.*

These two—John Claghorn and Lydia West—were married in 1770. Before a
year was over, both were dead.

Gay Head Light

Light List No. 630
41° 20.9' N, 70° 50.1 W
Ht. above water: 170 feet
Spider lamps; 10 Lewis lamps; 1st-order Fresnel (1856);
*   aerobeacons (1952)*
Built 1799; rebuilt 1856
Range: 24 miles
Alternating white and red flashes every 15 seconds
Red brick tower

Gay Head, like Sankaty Head and Highland, is a massive cliff. It is some 130 feet high at the western end of Martha's Vineyard. Famous for the different-colored strata of clay that form it, and for the fossils found there, it was an ideal place for a lighthouse.

It was State Senator Peleg Coffin of Nantucket who first wrote his Congressman suggesting that "the convenience and interest of Nantucket" would be aided by a light on Gay Head. The idea went to Alexander Hamilton, Secretary of the Treasury. After getting outside opinions, he requested $5750 from Congress; on July 16, 1798, the money was voted.

Events moved rapidly. In February, 1799, Massachusetts ceded just over two acres to the United States. The specifications, published on May 20, 1799, read in part:

**Figure 27.1   The 1856 Gay Head tower and double keepers'
house. National Archives photo.**

*The form is to be an octagon, the foundation to be of stone, sunk
three feet below the surface of the earth . . . The height of the
Pyramid is to be forty-seven feet from the stone work to the top of the
floor of the lantern; here the diameter is to be eight feet. . . . A
complete and sufficient Iron Lantern of six feet diameter, and in an
octagonal form, is to rest upon the Platform.*

A keeper's dwelling was also specified, seventeen feet by twenty-six feet,
with a parlor, bedroom, and kitchen. A barn, a well at least twenty feet deep,
and an underground oil storage vault completed the project.

The contract went to Martin Lincoln, son of General Benjamin Lincoln,
Boston collector of customs. Well before the required date of November 20
the entire project was completed—for $5750. Ebenezer Skiff, appointed the
first keeper, was warned by General Lincoln that "you must not become a
retailer of ardent spirits, for many people have informed [me] that a measure
of this kind would destroy the Indians." The light, with a revolving "eclipser"

every four minutes, had a number of spider lamps and was first lit on November 18, 1799.

In April, 1800, Skiff complained that his cellar was half-full of water for most of the spring. He also considered his salary quite inadequate. For two years he wrote his boss, the collector of customs in Boston, to no effect. So he went over his head to Albert Gallatin, Secretary of the Treasury. His arguments were apparently sound, for he received a $50 raise to $250 per year.

When Captain Winslow Lewis began maintaining and building lighthouses, out went the old lamps, and ten Lewis lamps with reflectors replaced them. This new technology was much more complex. Skiff complained again and received another $50 raise.

Finally, in January 1828, having spent twenty-nine years as keeper, Ebenezer Skiff retired, asking that his son Ellis replace him. Pleasonton concurred, and Ellis Skiff received his commission from President John Quincy Adams at a salary of $350 a year.

By 1838 the deck and lantern were so corroded that they were dangerous, and for once Pleasonton moved fast. In two months a blacksmith from New Bedford removed both and rebuilt them, and the light was back in operation. Meanwhile a substitute light was used.

Shortly after the repairs Lieutenant Carpender inspected the light:

Gay Head—Revolving—160 feet above sea level—four minute revolution, seen upwards of 20 miles. Lantern is seven feet high, seven feet wide, larger than is necessary. . . . Premises in good order.

This was the first written description of Gay Head.

During I.W.P. Lewis's inspection tour of 1842, he noted that the light was very weak and that "at the distance of 12 miles it is obscured about three-quarters of the time." He urged installation of a first-order Fresnel lens, then being tried out for the first time at the Navesink Light in New York. Twelve years later Gay Head had its lens.

National politics affected the Lighthouse Service. So when, for instance, James Polk, a Democrat, became president in 1845, Ellis Skiff was out and Samuel Flanders was in. The Skiffs had served a total of fifty-six years. How Ellis and his wife Keziah brought up their fourteen children there is a modern mystery.

In 1852 Congress established the professional Lighthouse Board, and

Figure 27.2 *City of Columbus* **wreck, January 19, 1884.
Courtesy of William P. Quinn.**

Stephen Pleasonton was relieved of responsibility after thirty years. The *Vineyard Gazette* crowed:

> *We are very glad to learn that Mr. Pleasonton has lost his office. It is astonishing that our Government has kept a regular antediluvian old Granny like Pleasonton in office for almost half a century.*

Pleasonton had planned to upgrade the light, and in 1854, new lamps and large reflectors went into the lantern. But two weeks later, on August 3, 1854, Congress voted $30,000 for a first-order Fresnel lens from France; in addition, a new brick tower, a double keepers' house, an oil house, and a barn were authorized. By the end of November, 1856, the work was done, and on December 1 the new lens shone forth, flashing every ten seconds. Later every fourth flash was red, according to the 1874 light list.

Among many others, the worst disaster off Gay Head was that of the *City of Columbus*. She piled up on a ledge at 4:00 A.M. on January 19, 1884. Almost everyone was asleep, and so in a few minutes 103 people drowned. Keeper

Figure 27.3   Gay Head from one mile south. From *Light House List, 1892*.

Horatio Pease of Gay Head rounded up a crew of Indians and on their second try reached the wreck. Pease yelled to the people on deck to jump into the water. Pulling them into the boat, he maneuvered the boat close to shore, where it capsized again; but all were saved. Other boats saved some twenty more. The captain, who survived, lost his license.

In 1890 Horatio Pease retired after twenty-seven years, and William Atchison relieved him. With this family ten years of mysterious illnesses beset the keepers. Causes could only be guessed at. Atchison, very ill, resigned in 1891. Edward Lowe took over in February 1891, and a year later he died at the age of forty-four.

In 1896 over a period of fifteen months, four of Keeper Crosby Crocker's children died. Finally in 1899, after forty-three years, the Lighthouse Board reported that: "The house is too damp and unsanitary for safe occupation by human beings." In 1902 the Board razed the dank brick house and replaced it with a gambrel-roofed wooden one, built well off the ground on a higher foundation.

Keeper Crocker retired in 1920, after thirty years. Charles Vanderhoop, the first Wampanoag Indian to become a keeper, replaced him and retired in 1933. Next came James Dolby, who died after four years, to be replaced by Frank Grieder, who was serving when the Coast Guard took over in 1939.

During World War II a small lamp dimmed the light, and when the war ended it resumed its former status. Meanwhile the station was still without running water or electricity. So Mrs. Elsie Grieder wrote President Truman, pointing out the disgraceful conditions under which they lived. It worked—but slowly. The Grieders retired and Joseph Hindley, the new keeper, had to wait until 1952 for the improvements.

Figure 27.4 "Ladies' Day" at Gay Head, 1910. Courtesy of Thornton Burgess Museum.

Final changes have been few. In 1950 a brick lookout tower was built, costing $16,000. Then two aerobeacons replaced the old lens, which may be seen today at the Dukes County Historical Society. In 1959 and 1961 the buildings at the station were demolished.

In 1986 a most unusual contract was drawn up. The Vineyard Environmental Research Institute received a contract to repair and maintain three lighthouses: Gay Head, East Chop, and Edgartown. The Coast Guard owns them and operates the lights.

The lighthouses have all been "victims of graffiti, broken glass, bullet holes, and broken doors," said the Institute's president, William Marks. The lease is automatically renewable for another thirty years. Thus a private organization (like many across the country) is helping to preserve a significant piece of the island's history.

In his newsletter of May, 1986, Congressman Gerry Studds wrote:

The most important lesson that emerged is that lighthouses can be saved, and protected from both natural and man-made dangers, if people are willing to put the time, money and effort into seeing that this is done.

Figure 27.5 Airview of the cliff and light station (undated). The edge is much nearer now. U.S. Coast Guard photo.

Principal Keepers at Gay Head

1799	Ebenezer Skiff	1890	William Atchison
1828	Ellis Skiff	1891	Edward P. Lowe
1845	Samuel Flanders	1892	Crosby L. Crocker
1849	Henry Robinson	1920	Charles W. Vanderhoop
1853	Samuel Flanders (again)	1933	James E. Dolby
1861	Ichabod Norton Luce	1937	Frank A. Grieder
1864	Calvin C. Adams	1948	Joseph Hindley
1869	Horatio N.T. Pease	1956	Light automated

Note

For this chapter I have relied heavily on Arthur Railton's "Gay Head Light" in the *Dukes County Intelligencer.*

28

Cape Poge Light

Light List No. 12915
41° 25.2' N, 70° 27.2' W
Ht. above water: 65 feet
Spider lamp; Lewis lamps; Fresnel lens (1857);
    300 mm optic today
Built 1801; rebuilt 1844, 1893
Moved 1838, 1893, 1907, 1986
Range: 9 miles
Flashing red every 4 seconds
White conical tower

*C*ape Poge is the northeast tip of Chappaquiddick Island, just east of Martha's Vineyard. A flat, sandy spit, with dunes and low scrub, it is a most desolate place. But it was a fine place for a lighthouse. So in 1801 the United States bought four acres at the tip for $30, and on January 30, 1801, Congress voted $2000 for a lighthouse and dwelling.

On August 1, 1801, specifications for the tower and house came out in the *New England Paladium*, reading in part:

> *The form is to be an Octagon; the foundation to be of stone, and sunk two feet below the surface of the ground. . . . The octagon pyramid to be of wood, good oak or white pine timber; to be 19 feet in diameter at the base thereof, the pyramid to be 35 feet high. . . . A*

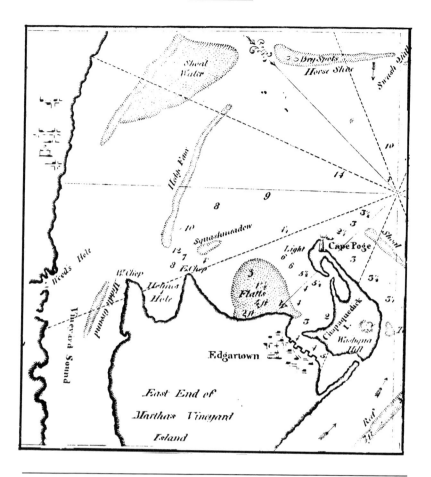

Figure 28.1   Earliest map showing Cape Poge Light in the possession of the Dukes County Historical Society (1809). Courtesy of the Society.

complete and sufficient Iron Lantern of 4½ feet diameter . . . is to rest on the platform. . . . The Lantern is to be five and a half feet high from the floor to the dome or roof.*

The keeper's frame house, fifteen by thirty-two feet, had one and a half stories, a six-foot-deep basement, and double chimneys.

---

* The size of the lantern was to cause trouble for the keepers for many years. It was simply so small (in both dimensions) that they could not work inside it and trim their lamps. This caused great breakage of glass lamp chimneys. The keepers had to work from outside to trim their lamps, and the wind blew the flame against the glass chimneys, breaking them.

By November, 1801, the work was completed. President Jefferson appointed Matthew Mayhew keeper, and late in December Mayhew, earning $200 a year, lit the lamp. He described it in a letter as "12 inches broad and 6 1/2 inches deep with eight nosses [noses, perhaps, meaning wicks in an old-fashioned spider lamp]." The lantern was fifty-five feet above the sea, showing a fixed white light.

In the fall of 1812 Captain Winslow Lewis refitted the lantern with his imitation Argand lamps. Soon Mayhew was asking for "sum mor tube glasses [lamp chimneys];" they kept breaking because of the size of the lantern.

On Lewis's inspection trip in 1815 he recommended adding a room to the keeper's house. Mayhew's family now included ten people living in that tiny house. Washington approved, and by October, 1816, the Mayhews were luxuriating in their larger house.

Finally the deck and lantern were so deteriorated that Lewis recommended rebuilding, with a larger lantern. A seven-foot-wide lantern allowed the keepers room for their work. Mayhew now received $350 a year, and for the first time he and other keepers were required to keep a daily journal and quarterly summary of important events.

Cape Poge suffers heavy erosion. In the spring of 1825 Mayhew wrote the collector of customs in Boston (his boss):

Takeing into view the situation . . . I think it my indispensible duty to acquaint you therewith, in the year 1800 there was of Land 4 acres, and now their is about 2 acres. . . .

He urged moving the house before it washed away. Pleasonton approved buying four more acres and moving the house.

After thirty-four years Matthew Mayhew died on December 20, 1834. Captain Lott Norton succeeded him, but he could not reach the station for two weeks "because of the ice." There is no record of who served meanwhile—probably the widow Mayhew. During that time the schooner *Hudson* came ashore on Cape Poge, and passengers and crew were lost.

When Carpender inspected the station in 1838, he observed that:

They were in the act of moving the tower (which is of wood) a few yards back. . . . This is an exceedingly useful light, not only as a guide to Edgartown harbor . . . but to the trade entering the "shoals" from the southward. . . .

Figure 28.2   The 1844 tower with the 1801 dwelling. Courtesy of the Dukes County Historical Society.

In 1842 I.W.P. Lewis's report on Cape Poge observed the tower "in a state of partial or complete ruin." Pleasonton moved very quickly and in June, 1844, approved building a new tower. Winslow Lewis, now seventy-three, did the job for $1600 for both tower and lamps, finishing before the contract's completion date of September 1.

Lott Norton, seventy-two, died on November 20, 1844. Quickly another Norton, Captain Aaron, replaced him, only to be ousted in 1848, when the Whigs reclaimed the White House. Edward Worth, a Whig, succeeded him. And so it went for many years.

Worth lasted until 1853, when Daniel Smith supplanted him. He in turn gave way to George Marchant in 1859. In 1866 Edward Worth was back as keeper, until 1882. In 1867 Cape Poge became a two-man station and Worth's pay went up to $565; his assistant received $400.

During the Civil War some twenty lighthouses suffered damage or

**Figure 28.3   The new (1880) double dwelling with the 1844
tower. Courtesy of the Dukes County Historical Society.**

destruction, and nearly all lights were darkened as a defense measure. But by
1866 things were back to normal. And (normally) the sea kept eating away at
the cape. By 1878 Keeper Worth reported that the house was thirty-six feet
from the edge of the cliff. That year the Lighthouse Board reported that:

> *It is probable that the keeper's dwelling will fall into the sea within
> two years. . . . Five thousand dollars will be required to build a
> double set of quarters for the two keepers.*

The new double house was ready by 1880, and the old house and barn
became the keepers' woodpile.

Improvements in conditions began to come. Keeper Worth's log of
February 23, 1881, records that the *Verbena* left "one library (No. 14)
[circulating boxes of books] for the use of the station." And he also received
the first full set of regulations, *Laws and Regulations Relating to the Lighthouse Establishment.* Shortly thereafter the log reads: "received one Medicine
Chest from the Inspector." And soon he received "a uniform suit, likewise a
working suit."

**Figure 28.4   Cape Poge showing cliff erosion. Courtesy of
William P. Quinn.**

By 1893 the sea was again reaching for the tower, and a "new temporary light tower . . . was built 40 feet distant from the old one." The old tower's lantern was moved over and the tower was demolished. This "temporary" tower is the one standing there today! In 1898 the light became flashing red and white instead of fixed white.

By 1901 there had been great strides in technology—and little improvement in living conditions. But in 1904 carpenters shingled the house, dug a new well (with a new hand pump) and cesspool, and installed water closets. In April 1905, the assistant keeper's son drowned, and in 1907 the tower had to be moved again. "Carpenters put down sand anchors against the powerful winds."

The bearings in the base of the lens began to give trouble as early as November 26, 1911. The keeper's log reads:

The revolving parts in lantern working very bad. Stopped four times last night, had to turn by hand. Sent to office for someone to come and fix it.

For four nights the keepers had to turn the lens by hand. Finally new bearings arrived on December 1, and the keepers installed them. Again in 1917 the lens seized up, and again they sweated through the night. The reason for the trouble was that the tower had settled out of plumb. That spring carpenters straightened the tower and installed new guy wires.

That winter of 1917 was vicious. The keepers had to gather driftwood to keep warm; their allowances of coal and wood had been exhausted. In addition the assistant keeper's wife had a baby daughter there, the first recorded birth at the station. In the spring the entire Hopkins family went to town for supplies—the first time Mrs. Hopkins had been off the station since the previous May.

Henry L. Thomas was keeper from 1919 to 1931. A hard taskmaster, he drove himself and his assistant to maintain the station. Perhaps he drove too hard, for several log entries in 1919 and 1920 report the assistant asleep on watch. He didn't last long. In 1921 Thomas lost his assistant and struggled on, not a well man, until he could struggle no more. The lens was still giving problems, and his wife was seriously ill. Finally he received orders to the more comfortable Edgartown Light, effective February 1, 1931.

The last keeper was Joseph Dubois, who reported in 1938. He too struggled on until October, 1943, when the light was automated as a fixed white flasher.

In 1954 Robert Marshall bought the buildings and tore them down for the lumber. In August, 1960, the tower was again moved back 150 feet. Then, in the spring of 1986 the tower was again moved (the seventh move for tower or house)—this time by heavy-lift helicopter.

Principal Keepers at Cape Poge

1801	Matthew Mayhew	1883	George H. Fisher
1835	Lott Norton	1898	George H. Dolby
1844	Aaron Norton	1902	Wallace Eldredge
1850	Edward Worth	1908	J.E. Barrus

1853	Daniel Smith	1919	Henry L. Thomas
1859	George Ripley Marchant	1931	Marcus Pieffer
1866	Edward Worth	1938	Joseph H. Dubois
1882	Jethro Worth	1943	Light automated

Note

For this chapter I lean heavily on Arthur Railton's "Cape Poge Light: Remote and Lonely" in the *Dukes County Intelligencer* of the Dukes County Historical Society.

Figure 28.5   The 1986 moving of the tower by helicopter. U.S. Coast Guard photo.

Holmes's Hole Light

Light List No. 12965
41° 28.8' N, 70° 36' W
Ht. above water: 84 feet
10 lamps; 4th-order Fresnel lens (1856)
Built 1817; rebuilt 1846, 1891
Range: 15 miles
Occulting white every 4 seconds, red sector 281° to 331°
White conical tower
Horn: 1 blast every 30 seconds

*H*olmes's Hole is the Vineyarders' name for the great harbor of Vineyard Haven. The two arms of land protecting the harbor are called East Chop and West Chop. This was the busiest harbor on the island.

Because of its importance, the citizens of Holmes's Hole (as the town was then called) felt that West Chop needed a lighthouse. So they asked their Congressman to have an appropriation enacted. He acted quickly, and on March 3, 1817, Congress approved $5000 "for building a light-house on the west chop of Holmes's Hole . . . and to furnish the same with all necessary supplies." On April 15, 1817, Abijah and Mary Luce sold the land for the light station for $225.

The contract went to Benjamin Beall and Duncan Thaxter for $4850.

Figure 29.1   Holmes's Hole 1817 light station. National Archives photo.

They built a stone tower twenty-five feet high, sixty feet above the sea, with ten Lewis-type lamps in an octagonal lantern, as well as "a stone dwelling House" thirty-four feet by twenty feet, with a porch. Thomas Cooke certified the work as complete on October 4, 1817, and on November 3 James West became keeper at the usual $300 per year.

The next year a boat was authorized for the station "and to have the slip made as recommended by him [West] provided the expense not to exceed $150," wrote Pleasonton. Aside from the problem of transportation for many stations, these boats frequently served as rescue craft. Often they were provided by the Boston Humane Society before founding of the Life-Saving Service.

Lieutenant Carpender's report in 1838 had this to say, in part:

I found this light in admirable order; reflectors bright, glass perfectly clean, lamps carefully trimmed, and everything justifying the high reputation it enjoys along the coast. The sea is encroaching. . . , [and]

I recommend that the light be placed about three hundred yards farther to the southward. . . . No less than 127 vessels have been ashore here during the twenty years this keeper has attended the light.

In 1843 Pleasonton approved adding a room to the two-room-and-kitchen house. And I.W.P. Lewis's inspection trip report pointed out the poor workmanship of the installation: rubble masonry laid up in bad lime, walls cracked and leaking, a loose and leaky soapstone roof on the tower, and rotten woodwork. He ended with this comment: "Present keeper deserves great praise for great neatness of the establishment."

In view of these conditions, in 1846 Pleasonton called for bids to rebuild both the house and the tower, to be completed by October 10, 1846. Abner and David West sold two acres and three rods of land for the new location, about 975 feet southeast of the old location—just about the distance Carpender had recommended eight years before. On October 13 Keeper West certified the work as completed by Marshall Lincoln at a cost of $2329. A new lantern built by Winslow Lewis for $635 surmounted the new tower.

But James West had little time to enjoy his new quarters, for he resigned

Figure 29.2   The new 1846 tower and dwelling. In front is the 1882 fog-whistle building. Courtesy of William P. Quinn.

in 1847, after thirty years at the light, and Charles West became keeper. That September Pleasonton wrote Pease, Vineyard collector of customs, telling him to procure new lamps and reflectors on bid. Winslow Lewis, still going strong, had the lowest bid of $475, which was accepted. The new lamps were lit on January 28, 1848.

In 1854 three beacons or "bug lights" were proposed to serve as a range for vessels entering the harbor. Quickly built, they began service on December 4, 1854. A keeper's house followed and was completed six months later. But in 1856 the bug lights were discontinued and replaced by a fourth-order Fresnel lens in a lantern on the beacon-keeper's house. Then in December 1859, this light, "having been deemed useless, was discontinued."* In 1872, after the lantern was removed and stored at the Woods Hole Depot, the land and buildings were sold at auction.

Changes in the next few years were routine maintenance, but in 1882 "A frame engine house was erected, and a steam-whistle established for a fog signal. A one-and-one-half story frame dwelling [for the assistant keeper] was erected."

Finally, in 1888, "the dilapidated stone dwelling of 1817 was torn down and a frame house built upon its foundation." The next year a red sector was inserted into the fixed white light to cover Squash Meadow and Norton's Shoals. The original site of the light (about three acres) went at auction for $650.

In 1891 some nearby houses were obscuring part of the light, and so an iron mast seventeen feet high was attached to the lantern, with the lens at the top. The next year the old 1846 tower of rubble masonry, covered with shingles because of its poor condition, was demolished. A new red brick tower, forty-five feet high, rose on the old foundation.

As kerosene became the fuel of choice (because of its cheapness and burning qualities), an oil house was built for safe storage of this volatile fuel. And then in 1896, after seventy-nine years, "city water was furnished to the keeper's dwellings." In 1899 the red brick tower was painted white.

The twentieth century saw few changes. In 1925 a metal garage was built at a cost of $300, and in 1943 an eight-foot-square lookout tower (since demolished) was built for $950. The last improvement to the property was another garage, built in 1966, of wood with a clapboard finish. The light is now automated, although Coast Guard personnel live in the quarters.

Today West Chop shows an occulting (more light than darkness) white light every four seconds, with the same red sector over the two shoals.

---

*Quotations here are from various Lighthouse Board reports.

**Figure 29.3   Holmes's Hole Light today, from the water.
Photo in August, 1990, by Dr. Richard Sommers.**

Edgartown Light

Light List No. 14085
41° 23.5' N, 70° 30.2' W
Ht. above water: 45 feet
10 lamps; 4th-order Fresnel lens (1856); 250 mm optic
Built 1828
Demolished 1941; Ipswich tower moved to replace it
Range: 5 miles
Flashing red every 6 seconds
White conical tower today

*E*dgartown Light, on the edge of the harbor formed by the east side of the Vineyard and the west side of Cuttyhunk, had its beginning with an act of Congress on May 23, 1828, appropriating $5500 and stating:

> *That the Secretary of the Treasury be empowered to provide, by contract, for building a pier and light-house on the Point of Flats, at the entrance to Edgartown Harbor, in the state of Massachusetts.*

In June Henry Dearborn, Boston Collector of Customs, advertised for bids, giving specifications for the lighthouse, to be fitted with ten lamps and fourteen-inch reflectors. The design chosen was that of a two-story house

Figure 30.1   First Edgartown Light (photo ca. 1880). Courtesy of the Dukes County Historical Society.

with the tower and lantern projecting from the roof. On July 30 the government bought a small piece of beach from Seth Vincent for $80.

Then complications arose because the appropriation was not adequate for the difficult location; it required the driving of pilings into the shifting sand. Only one bid was received, from Winslow Lewis, and Dearborn wrote Fifth Auditor Pleasonton a puzzled letter on July 9, 1828:

> *For the Pier, Light, and Dwelling House $3450. Crossway: $2750, Fitting $385. . . . Shall I contract with him, for the crossway also or only for the pier Lighthouse and fitting up? He is willing to complete the whole and wait for the requisite additional appropriations to be made.*

The house with the lantern on the roof, sitting on a stone pier, was soon completed, but the keeper had to row to shore until 1830. That year a

Congressional vote of $2500 provided for the causeway to shore, which the *Vineyard Gazette* described thus:

> *It ran straight to the shore landing to the north of the old salt works. It was built in box shape, i.e. the lower part boarded in with hemlock boards spiked to spiles. . . . Damage was often sustained, also, by ice.*

Jeremiah Pease, the first keeper, was a man of many talents. His diary is being published serially by the Dukes County Historical Society. In May 1825, we find him setting the broken arm of William Holley, who fell off a windmill vane. In June he receives $2.50 for surveying land at Cape Poge for the lighthouse. He draws up deeds, drafts plot plans, acts as an accountant.

He spent thirteen years in the comfortable (for a change) dwelling, drawing $300 a year. An odd event occurred on November 16, 1841, the year of the smallpox plague. Thomas M. Mayhew visited the station that day and died the next day of the disease, according to Pease's diary.

Edward Carpender's inspection report of November 1, 1838, had a lot to say about the light:

> *This light is on the keeper's dwelling, at the end of a short wooden breakwater in the harbor of Edgartown. Cape Poge Light, 4 miles outside, is the guide to the harbor. so that the light on the breakwater requires to be of little magnitude; yet I found the same number of lamps here as in the most exposed situations in the district. . . . It cannot be long before Government will have to reconstruct this breakwater and Light-house, as the worms [teredo or shipworms] have made great havoc with them, and the sea threatens them . . . with total destruction.*

But ice and water did greater damage to the walkway. On December 6, 1830, forty feet of the walkway were carried away by ice; repairs were made that summer. Again in January 1836, a bad storm did serious damage. In March 1850, Congress voted another $5000 to build a breakwater of rock, with the walkway on its top. Frequently since then the wooden parts have had to be replaced.

A report of 1842 stressed the importance of the harbor:

> *Edgartown harbor is the only safe one, accessible at low water, in the Vineyard sound; and this harbor will in a few years be so filled*

*up as to become useless. . . . A breakwater, of 1,200 feet in length, is
required to keep the sand and silt from washing into the harbor.*

Jeremiah Pease (a Democrat) was eventually "bumped" from his station
by the spoils system in 1841. Sylvanus Crocker (a Whig) held the post from
1841 to 1843, when Pease again became keeper. But in 1849 there was
another shift in power in Washington, and Crocker came in again. Pease was
not at all happy about the situation and wrote in his diary on April 25, 1849:

*This day I am again removed from Keeper of Edgartown Light
House under Gen. Taylor's Administration, notwithstanding his
many pledges, declarations, etc., etc. Silvanus Crocker is again
appointed in my stead. Attended the discharging of said Brig* [Blue
Nose] *at H. Hole.*

After 1852, when the Lighthouse Board was formed, appointments were no
longer political. But keepers did not stay long. William Vinson lasted two
years and James Blankenship six. William Vincent was keeper for five years,
followed by Zolmond Steward, and Benjamin Huxford took over in 1870.

On April 18, 1856, the *Vineyard Gazette* reported on a fire in the
keeper's house: "It was caused by the boiling over of a kettle of varnish which
was placed on the stove. The damage was very trifling."

During the late 1860's extensive repairs and renovations occurred:
rooms were repapered; two iron smokestacks were raised; sills of the house
were replaced; the house was whitewashed; and the walkway was again
repaired.

The 1890's saw other improvements. First a fuel and store house twenty-
eight feet by nine feet was built, and a close board fence 182 feet long
replaced the old fence around the pier. A new well was driven, and the next
year an iron oil house was built to hold the new fuel, kerosene.

Henry L. Thomas, who spent twelve years at Cape Poge, finally had his
request for transfer accepted and became keeper at Edgartown on February
1, 1931. The light source was still a 480-candlepower Aladdin lamp, fueled by
kerosene; electricity had not yet come to the station, even though it was just
offshore. The problem, apparently, was that walkway and its nearly annual
destruction.

After their previous isolated stations (Plymouth, Great Point, and Cape
Poge) the Thomases enjoyed the modern conveniences of a radio, a good
heating system, and town water. Henry also had a fog bell, operated by

clockworks, which rang every fifteen seconds in heavy weather. He retired in 1938.

The old house, after 111 years and the 1938 hurricane, was in very poor condition. One of the first acts of the Coast Guard (which assumed control of the Lighthouse Service in 1939) was to demolish the old building. To replace it they dismantled the much newer cast iron Essex Light in Ipswich, shipped it by barge to Edgartown, and reassembled it close to the original site.

This lighthouse is also maintained by the Vineyard Environmental Research Institute. It now flashes red every six seconds from its white conical tower forty-five feet high. Edward Carpender had strongly recommended making Edgartown Light red a century earlier.

The list of keepers is fairly complete except for a large gap between 1870 and 1919. No record is available for that period.

List of Keepers

1828	Jeremiah Pease	1866	Zolmond Steward
1841	Sylvanus Crocker	1870	Benjamin Huxford
1843	Jeremiah Pease		(from the 1870 census)
1849	Sylvanus Crocker	1919	Joseph H. Barrus
1853	William Vinson	1931	Henry L. Thomas
1855	James Blankenship	1938	Fred Vidler
1861	William Vincent		

Figure 30.2   The new tower (from Ipswich) and Keeper Benjamin Ellsworth, commissioned by President Lincoln, 1861. Courtesy of Dukes County Historical Society.

Figure 30.3   The new tower from the water, July, 1990. Photo by Dr. Richard Sommers.

East Chop Light

Light List No. 12945
41° 28.2' N, 70° 34.1' W
Ht. above water: 79 feet
3 lamps; 4th-order Fresnel lens (1856); 300 mm. optic
Built 1869 (privately); rebuilt 1872, 1878
Range: 9 miles
Equal green and dark every 6 seconds
White tower

*E*ast Chop Light is located on Telegraph Hill on the eastern point of Vineyard Haven harbor. Originally a telegraph station occupied the site. Beginning in 1828, Jonathan Grout, Jr., operated a semaphore tower there, part of a system of stations linking Nantucket, Edgartown, East Chop, Woods Hole, West Falmouth, and Boston. Their purpose was to announce to Boston ship arrivals at the islands. In 1834 the semaphore station was discontinued.

Then in 1869 Captain Silas Daggett built a private lighthouse there, which lasted seven years. In the *Vineyard Gazette* of June 11, 1869, this NOTICE TO MARINERS appeared:

> *The undersigned has at a considerable expense erected a light-house . . . on the East Chop. . . . The height of the lantern above the sea is about sixty feet from which a fixed RED LIGHT will be*

**Figure 31.1   East Chop Light ca. 1903. Courtesy of Dukes
County Historical Society.**

exhibited on and after June 5. Captains, Owners, and Underwriters of vessels cannot fail to appreciate the convenience of this light and should therefore be willing to contribute to its support.

The government loaned Captain Daggett three twenty-one-inch reflectors in 1871. In December the lighthouse burned to the ground while Captain Grafton Luce was keeper. But by May, 1872, it had been rebuilt and relighted, showing the fixed red light. The 1874 *List of Lights* describes the light: "A FIXED RED light is exhibited from the tower on a one-story Mansard-roofed white house." The lantern was sixty-eight feet above the sea.

After considerable urging that the lighthouse should be acquired by the United States, on March 3, 1876, Congress authorized $5000 to purchase the property. Silas Daggett sold his lighthouse on May 30, 1876, for $3562.50. The 1877 Lighthouse Board reports that:

This station . . . was purchased by the government last year . . . and the building, purchased with the land, which served as a keeper's

> *dwelling and for displaying the light, was a slight wooden structure,*
> *little better than a shanty. A new dwelling and cast iron tower [like*
> *Chatham's] . . . will soon be completed.*

While construction was going on, a fourth-order lens in a temporary tower displayed the red light. The 1878 report tells of completion of the tower and frame dwelling, which were both painted white. A fixed red light shone from the new tower. At some time between 1874 and 1898 the light became fixed white.

The years at East Chop were quiet ones, with mostly routine maintenance reported by the Lighthouse Board. In 1897 an oil house (reflecting the growing use of volatile kerosene) was built, and in 1898 the report says: "The fixed white light was improved by changing it to flashing red."

Today the only structure remaining is the cast iron tower. It too is maintained by the Vineyard Environmental Research Institute, under contract with the Coast Guard. The tower, which was brown for many years, is now white and shows a three-second green flashing light every six seconds.

Figure 31.2 East Chop Light. From *Light House List, 1891*.

Figure 31.3 East Chop Light today. Courtesy of *Cape Cod Times*.

Cuttyhunk Island and Light

Light List No. 14235
41° 24.8' N, 70° 57' W
Ht. above water: 63 feet
9 lamps; Fresnel lens (1857); 300 mm optic
Built 1823; rebuilt 1860, 1892
Range: 12 miles
Quick flashing white
White skeleton tower replaced 1892 tower in 1947

Cuttyhunk—an English approxima-
tion of the Wampanoag name Poocutohhunkkunnah—was the first place in
the New World colonized by Englishmen, if only for three weeks.
Bartholomew Gosnold decided that the island was an ideal place for a
settlement, and in May 1602 he and his crew of thirty-one built a fort, writes
Gabriel Archer, on a pond,

> *in curcuit two miles, on the one side not distant from the sea thirty*
> *yards, in the center whereof is a rocky islet, containing near an acre*
> *of ground full of wood, on which we began our fort and place of*
> *abode.*

They explored nearby islands and the mainland and planted crops on
Martha's Vineyard. And they greatly enjoyed the bountiful seafood: "Scallops,

Figure 32.1   Gosnold's men at Cuttyhunk. From Amelia Forbes Emerson, *Early History of Naushon Island*.

Muscles, Cockles, Lobsters, Crabs, Oisters, and Wilks [Whelks], exceeding good and great." But the best find was sassafras, the most expensive medicine in England. So they loaded the *Concord* with sassafras and cedar for their return to England.

In early June they had a visit from nine canoes of Indians with their sachem. They gave the Indians a fish dinner, which their guests enjoyed, and "They misliked nothing but our mustard, whereat they made a sowre face," says Archer.

But a few days later the Wampanoags ambushed the group, wounding one man. As a result, while Gosnold had planned to leave a colony there, the risk seemed too great. So the whole company embarked for England, arriving on July 23, 1602. The foundations of the fort were seen as late as 1797. So ended the first "colony" in New England.

The island remained merely an Indian hunting and fishing ground for many years. In due course it was part of the Thomas Mayhew purchase in

1641 (See Chapter 22 for details). Then in 1654 Mayhew and his son purchased the Wampanoag rights, and in 1668 Peleg Sanford, Philip Smith, and Thomas Ward bought both Cuttyhunk and its neighbor Nashawena from the Mayhews.

The three proprietors accepted a fourth, Ralph Earle of Dartmouth, and divided their holdings. That same year Sanford sold Earle half his land, some 224 acres, for 100 pounds. In 1693 Peleg Slocum, a Quaker, bought out Earle and Sanford for 335 pounds. So in fifty years one small island sold for over ten times the forty pounds Mayhew had paid for *all* of the islands!

By that time we know that at least one family lived on Cuttyhunk. Ralph Earle, Jr.'s deed to Slocum mentions a house and fences. So we may assume that he was the first permanent resident on the island.

Peleg Slocum probably never lived there. But he pastured his sheep there and began farming, with Slocum relatives as tenants. Since all travel had to be by boat, Slocum's shallop (a small, open sailboat) covered many miles to and from Dartmouth, where he lived.

In 1691 an act of the Massachusetts General Court made the entire Elizabeth Islands chain part of Dukes County and of Chilmark on the Vineyard. This absentee rule caused great resentment, especially when the islands' Quakers refused to pay the "priest's rate" in 1724 to build a church in Chilmark. In retaliation the men of Chilmark raided Cuttyhunk and made off with some eighty cows, horses, and sheep. In fact, the islanders did not achieve their freedom until 1864, when the town of Gosnold on the island was incorporated.

The island stayed in the hands of the Slocums until 1864, when the Cuttyhunk Fishing Club (New York millionaires) bought most of it. In 1921 William Wood, president of the American Woolen Company, bought out the Cuttyhunk Fishing Club.

There was undoubtedly a school on the island. In any case, in 1754 Chilmark voted four pounds to build one for the growing crop of children there. The first record of population in 1761 lists "near twenty families on the island"—some ninety people. In 1777 there were seventeen families, and the 1790 census lists thirteen. On Nashawena there were ten families and twenty-one people on Pasque Island.

Perhaps the most notable American born on the island was Paul Cuffee, born to a black slave in 1750. He became a distinguished sea captain, builder and owner of ships, merchant who amassed a large fortune, and finally founder of Sierra Leone on the African west coast. His ships carried free black Americans there and gave logistic support.

The Elizabeth Islands, with their small and largely Quaker populations, played no active role in the Revolution or War of 1812. They were victims of British raids for supplies (especially livestock), and British sea patrols nearly stopped water transportation, so that often the islands were close to starvation.

Negotiations for the lighthouse began on May 7, 1822, with an appropriation by Congress of $3000. Massachusetts ceded its rights, and the Slocums sold "in consideration of $300 . . . a parcel of land containing 3 acres and 139 rods, bounded by the sea and a pond . . . , by a stone wall and the land of Christopher Slocum."

In August the government published specifications in the New Bedford *Mercury* for a lighthouse and dwelling 34' by 20', both of stone. The two-room house was to have a fireplace in each room, a porch (the kitchen), an outhouse, and a well.

The contract went to Deacon Nathan Davis of Somerset, who brought the stone over from the mainland in his sloop *Temperance*. Apparently he was a better Baptist preacher than lighthouse builder. When Edward Carpender inspected in 1838 he wrote:

> *This tower was originally of stone, but was so badly built as to require twice to be encased in brick. . . . This is one of those lights that require to be of extraordinary magnitude, and to be well attended.*

He sharply criticized the maintenance of the ten lamps and reflectors.

I.W.P. Lewis's inspection trip of 1842 led to a scathing report of the condition of Cuttyhunk Light, which was "a rubble stone tower . . . [which] is leaky, from the original error of using soapstone slabs for a roof, while the wood work of the keeper's house is rotten in every part."

The 1854 *Lights of the United States* lists Cuttyhunk as "On the southwest point of Cuttyhunk island, entrance to Buzzards Bay." Forty-two feet above sea level, the light showed fixed white from nine lamps, with a range of twelve miles. In 1857 Cuttyhunk and nineteen other lights in the Second District received Fresnel lenses.

In 1860 a major reconstruction took place. The keeper's dwelling received a second story, with the tower projecting from the roof. This was a very late use of this faulty design. The tower was now ten feet higher. But the elements kept gnawing away at the station, as shown by Lighthouse Board reports of the late 1860's. By 1881 "The Dwelling house and tower are in a dilapidated condition and require renovation."

Figure 32.2   The second Cuttyhunk Light (1860). U.S. Coast Guard photo.

A grim reminder of lighthouse life comes from the logs of S. Austin Smith, keeper from 1864 to 1881. No doctor was available; Mrs. Smith had been bedridden for seventeen days; and he was sick as well. And the light demanded its due as he tried to care for his family:

> *2/9/64   Employed in the house taking care of my sick family.*
>
> *2/13/64   Employed washing, cooking, cleaning the light. This is lonesome. We are all sick.*
>
> *2/27/64   We are now getting along more comfortably, as my wife can walk about now. Myself is much better of our sickness.*

Captain Smith's last mention in the log is by his replacement, William Atchison:

*10/24/81   ENE to NE Pm blowing strong. Mr. S. Austin Smith
and wife left this morning.*

Atchison too soon had his problems with the poor conditions:

*11/9/81   SW thick, Smoky with fresh Br PM Blowing hard
with rain. the tower leaks Bad Moping up water all
the afternoon and Spreading Cloths to Ketch the
Water so as to Save the Plaster from being Destroyed.*

Eventually something was done about these miserable conditions, but not
until 1892, when Captain Alfred G. Eisener was keeper. The *Evening
Standard* reported on August 29, 1891:

*The light-house . . . is to be taken down and the light moved to the
round tower now under process of construction. The new tower is of
wood with a stone foundation. . . . The light is a Fresnel of the fifth
order of lens.*

The new dwelling was to be much grander, too, of six rooms, with dormers
and a piazza. Downstairs would be a parlor, dining room, and kitchen, with
a hall and pantry. Upstairs would be three bedrooms. The article ended with:
"The work will probably be finished by October."

Captain Eisener (1849–1937), like many of his generation, went to sea,
becoming a shipmaster before joining the Lighthouse Service. And like so
many of his fellow keepers he was often called upon to risk his life to save
others' lives.

For example, the Canadian schooner *Rob and Harry* came ashore in a
terrible storm on March 11, 1892. He, his wife and daughter, and two
islanders launched the Humane Society boat and fought their way to the
wreck; two men jumped into the boat. But the line to the ship parted, and
they washed ashore, with the boat stove in. Eisener went for tools and timber
to repair it.

Meanwhile Captain Bosworth and his Life-Saving Station crew arrived
and helped repair the boat. Again they made it to the wreck and rescued the
two remaining men, one dead. Eisener paid for the burial and eventually was
reimbursed by Canada. He also received a silver Life-Saving Medal and $20.

The last keeper was Octave Ponsart. He and his wife comforted the
homesick soldiers stationed there during World War II with good food. Their

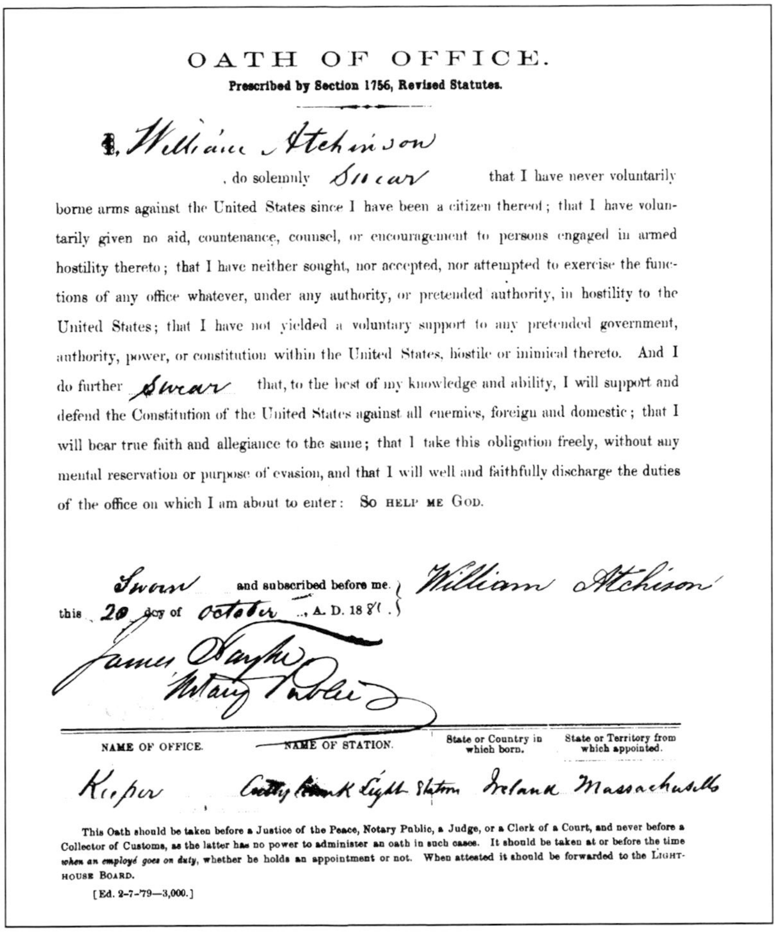

OATH OF OFFICE.

Prescribed by Section 1756, Revised Statutes.

I, *William Atchinson*

, do solemnly *Swear* that I have never voluntarily borne arms against the United States since I have been a citizen thereof; that I have voluntarily given no aid, countenance, counsel, or encouragement to persons engaged in armed hostility thereto; that I have neither sought, nor accepted, nor attempted to exercise the functions of any office whatever, under any authority, or pretended authority, in hostility to the United States; that I have not yielded a voluntary support to any pretended government, authority, power, or constitution within the United States, hostile or inimical thereto. And I do further *Swear* that, to the best of my knowledge and ability, I will support and defend the Constitution of the United States against all enemies, foreign and domestic; that I will bear true faith and allegiance to the same; that I take this obligation freely, without any mental reservation or purpose of evasion, and that I will well and faithfully discharge the duties of the office on which I am about to enter: So HELP ME GOD.

Sworn and subscribed before me. *William Atchison*

this 20 day of *October*, A. D. 188(.)

James Naylor
Notary Public

NAME OF OFFICE.	NAME OF STATION.	State or Country in which born.	State or Territory from which appointed.
Keeper	Cuttyhunk Light Station	Ireland	Massachusetts

This Oath should be taken before a Justice of the Peace, Notary Public, a Judge, or a Clerk of a Court, and never before a Collector of Customs, as the latter has no power to administer an oath in such cases. It should be taken at or before the time when an employé goes on duty, whether he holds an appointment or not. When attested it should be forwarded to the LIGHT-HOUSE BOARD.

[Ed. 2-7-79—3,000.]

Figure 32.3 Keeper William Atchison's oath of office.
National Archives photo.

daughter, Seamonde, was desolated when, as a child, she saw her new doll, dropped by the Flying Santa, lying broken on the rocks.

She wrote Edward Rowe Snow (the Santa), telling him of the tragedy. The next year Snow arrived by helicopter and handed her a lovely new doll. And every year until he died, she wrote him a Christmas letter. She grew up and became a Coast Guard officer.

In 1947 the Coast Guard disestablished the light. They tore down the tower and dwelling and built a skeleton tower nearby. The new light became

**Figure 32.4   The third Cuttyhunk Light. Courtesy of
William P. Quinn.**

group flashing white (two every ten seconds). In 1965 the characteristic became occulting white every five seconds.

Recent changes include battery power, with a wind-generator. And the light is now quick flashing white, sixty-three feet above the sea, with a range of twelve miles.

The Ponsarts retired, remaining on Cuttyhunk for many years. He is buried there, among those who have lost their lives at sea. On his tombstone is carved a lighthouse—a fitting memorial for Cuttyhunk's last lighthouse keeper.

Note

For this chapter I lean heavily on material provided by (and largely written by) Janet Bosworth, Curator of the Cuttyhunk Historical Society.

Naushon Island and Tarpaulin Cove Light

Light List No. 14200
41° 28.1' N, 70° 45.5' W
Ht. above water: 78 feet
10 lamps; 4th-order Fresnel lens (1856); 250 mm optic
Built (private) 1759; rebuilt 1818; 1891
Range: 9 miles
Flashing white every 6 seconds
White tower, small attached house

*N*aushon Island is the longest and largest of the Elizabeth Islands, which run south-southwest and separate Vineyard Sound from Buzzards Bay. Its first appearance in history is in the accounts of Brereton and Archer, members of Gosnold's 1602 expedition.

It is from John Brereton that we get an early clear glimpse of the original inhabitants:

These people as they are exceeding courteous, gentle of disposition,
excelling all others that we have seen; so for shape and bodily favor,
I think they excel all people of America; of stature much higher than
we; of complexion or color like a dark olive; their eyebrows and hair

*black, which they wear long, tied up in knots, whereon they prick
feathers of fowls.*

Naushon was included in Thomas Mayhew's purchase of the islands in
1641. It was not until 1654 that he negotiated with the island's sachem, Saeyk,
for land rights on "Cataymucke," Naushon's native name. Settlement was
slow, consisting mostly of Mayhew tenant farmers and herders. Finally, in
1682, the Mayhews sold the island to Wait Winthrop, grandson of John
Winthrop, first governor of the Massachusetts Bay Colony.

Winthrop held the island until 1730, before selling "Catamock or
Tarpolin Cove Island, Nonamesset, and adjacent islands" to Governor James
Bowdoin. That family owned the island for 113 years, until 1843. Governor
William Swain and John Murray Forbes bought it from Bowdoin College and
James Temple Bowdoin. Swain sold out to Forbes in 1856, and since then the
Forbes family have owned the island, which is now administered by a trust.

Naushon boasts the fourth light built on our coast, after Boston Light
(1716), Beaver Tail off Newport (1740), and Brant Point (1746), built by the
town of Nantucket. Tarpaulin Cove Light was also built privately by Zaccheus
Lumbert, formerly of Nantucket, in 1759. In addition he kept the tavern at the
cove and maintained the light, thanks to Nantucketers providing the "Oyle
out of their own courtesy."

Three years later he petitioned Governor Francis Bernard for some relief
from the expense of maintaining the light with these words:

*Zacchues Lumbert . . . Innholder [showeth] that he hath for the
public good of Whalemen and Coasters built a Lighthouse at said
Cove . . . [which] has been the means of saving many vessels from
being lost . . . , he hopes that your Excellency will make him an
allowance . . . that he may be excused from paying any Duty of
Exision on the liquors he sells.*

The governor ordered that he be paid six pounds! He kept up his light until
1764, when he gave up the tavern. The various tavern keepers may have
maintained the light until 1818, when the government bought it.

Like the other islands, Naushon had a different political development
from, say, Cape Cod and other Massachusetts locations. Here, for example,
four families have owned the whole island for 350 years. So there was no
sense of a commonwealth as represented by the Mayflower Compact, signed
in Cape Cod Bay by members of the Plymouth Colony.

**Figure 33.1   The wreck of the *Perseverance* in 1805. From
Amelia Forbes Emerson, *Early History of Naushon Island*.**

Farming and sheep-herding on the island were carried on by tenants for
most of the island's history. And because of their isolation, participation in
politics was nearly impossible. For over a hundred years Naushon was part of
Chilmark on the Vineyard, far away by water.

Ships' logs and shipping records reveal that Tarpaulin Cove was a busy
little harbor. Visitors of all kinds spent the night at the Tarpaulin Inn (later
Cove House). Often several ships at once were anchored there, and the
tavern rang with gaiety. The cove was also a natural market for the local
farmers, selling to the ships.

Of course there were many shipwrecks through the years. One disaster
was that of the ship *Perseverance*, which ran ashore at the cove on January
31, 1805. The first published report was in the *Columbian Centinel* of
February 2:

> *By Telegraph. The ship* Perseverance, *Capt. Cook, 135 days from
> Batavia is ashore in Tarpaulin Cove and bilged.* They want assis-
> tance! *(Jan. 31)*

**Figure 33.2   The first government-built Tarpaulin Cove
Light. National Archives photo.**

The newspaper went on to tell the story of the ship, built in 1794 in Haverhill, of 245 tons. Richard Wheatland, the first captain, made several voyages to Archangel in Russia and to China. In 1799 he met a french privateer which tried to capture his ship. After an hour-long gun battle the *Perseverance* crew beat off the Frenchman. Wheatland's account of the fight is in the *History of Essex County:*

> *While our guns loaded with round shot and square bars of iron six inches long were plied so briskly . . . that before he got out of range we had cut his mainsail and fore topsail all to rags and cleared his decks effectively so that there were scarce ten men to be seen.*

Wheatland retired and James Cook assumed command. On his way back from Batavia the wreck occurred. Fortunately, no lives were lost, and the cargo of coffee and sugar was saved. The ship was a total loss.

The island's proprietors were powerful. Because James Bowdoin opposed government acquisition of the lighthouse, there was an eleven-year delay between appropriation of funds in 1807 and action in 1818. He wrote many letters fighting the move, to Albert Gallatin, John Winthrop, and others.

He offered to give the government land for a lighthouse and proposed that "the public interest may be benefited by employing my tenant as keeper of the light house & in that case much expense and trouble might be saved to the public." His opposition prevailed, and the project was delayed until after his death.

On June 12, 1817, Massachusetts ceded land for the lighthouse. In November the United States bought land for $216, and construction (at a cost of $6062.11) could begin. The tower, thirty-eight feet high and nineteen feet in diameter at the base, and keeper's house were of rubble stone. With the usual array of lamps, eighty feet above the sea, the fixed white light had a range of thirteen miles. Amelia Forbes Emerson's *Naushon Data* lists John Geyer as the first keeper.

Edward Carpender inspected in 1838 and wrote: "This is an inland light. . . . I must continue to recommend the reduction of these lights to the want of navigation." He also reported that the reflectors were defaced by the use of too short chimneys and that the stone dwelling was defective.

When I.W.P. Lewis inspected the light in 1842, he reported that "The establishments at . . . Cape Poge, Tarpaulin Cove, and Gay Head were found in a state of partial or complete ruin and all require rebuilding." The tower leaked from top to bottom, and the keeper had to chip ice off the staircase in winter. And the well was dry.

Finally in 1845 permission was granted to dig a new well, and we know what it cost from Geyer's logs. Francis Burt and William Cummings dug the well for thirty-five days at $1.50 a day, and Tristram Cleveland took twenty-four days at $1.50 to build the well. Geyer notes: "What Mr. Cummings done to it last fall was of no use." He seems to have spent more time leaning on his shovel than digging.

John Geyer's annual report of supplies used includes 195 gallons of summer oil, 130 gallons of winter oil, 133 tube glasses (chimneys), and eight and one-half gross of wicks—over 1200 that year. Two years later he used only 180 wicks and twenty-four tube glasses. His pay in 1846 was $87.50 per quarter, or $350 per year.

In 1856 when Nathan Clifford was keeper, new Fresnel lenses were ordered for Tarpaulin Cove, Cape Poge, and West Chop. The manufacturer, Sautier et Cie. of Paris, provided them at 2604.5 francs each.

The heavy maintenance that these stations required is well illustrated by the Lighthouse Board report of 1868:

89. Tarpaulin Cove.—Wooden addition, 9 × 15, to dwelling built; new plank platform laid; privy repaired and reshingled on two sides; boat-house roof patched and renailed, and doors refitted; eaves of dwelling reshingled; two doors refitted and window sash and cellar case repaired; . . . The boat-house is very much in need of repair, and it is proposed to build a new one next year. A covered walk from the tower to the dwelling is also needed.

There were too many fixed white lights nearby. So when the new fifth-order lens went in on April 7, the characteristic became fixed white with a brilliant flash every thirty seconds.

Keepers came and went. After Nathan Clifford came Abraham White in 1861, followed by Samuel and William Skiff. In 1871 Captain Richard Norton, who lost his ship in the Civil War to the Confederate raider *Alabama*, became keeper. At that time both tower and house were painted white.

At last in 1888 something was done about the dilapidated, leaky stone house of 1818. The Board demolished it and on its foundation built a two-story house, 25' × 26', with an ell and a basement. Cost: $3000.

Soon the tower, too, came down. It had been in such poor condition that during the Civil War it had been shingled. In 1891 a new brick tower, twenty-eight feet high, with a new fourth-order lens, took its place. A 1200-pound fog-bell and bell tower were installed. From April 25 to June 30, 1891, the light shone from a temporary structure.

The quiet years came and went—with fewer wrecks—until the 1938 hurricane, which devastated New England. It demolished the thirty-foot bell tower, which was not replaced. Finally, on September 4, 1941, Tolman Spencer, keeper since 1928, gave up his post and the light was automated. Since then it has been maintained by the Woods Hole Coast Guard Depot.

By 1958 the light was considered less important, and its candlepower was reduced from 7,500 to 700. Then in 1962 the house and other buildings were in a "state of collapse" and were torn down. In 1967 the Fresnel lens was upgraded to fourth-order, and since then it has been replaced by a 200 mm lantern. Today the light, seventy-eight feet above sea level, flashes white every six seconds, with a range of nine miles.

In her *Naushon Data* Amelia Forbes Emerson lists all the keepers of the light, with some discrepancies from other sources:

1759–1764   Zaccheus Lumbert
1764–1817   Cove Tavern keepers

Figure 33.3   The new dwelling and tower (1891). Courtesy of the Thornton Burgess Museum.

1818	John Geyer
1852	Joseph R. Luce
1853	Nathan Clifford, Jr.
1861	Abraham C. White
1864	Samuel E. Skiff
1869	William E. Skiff
1871	Richard Norton
1882	Calvin N. Adams
1886	Frank S. Carson
1910	George A. Howard
1912	Frederick W. Field
1916	Carl Hill
1920	Frank Davis
1928–1941	Tolman Spencer, last keeper of the light

Figure 33.4   Tarpaulin Cove Light today. Airview courtesy of Wally Welch, *Lighthouses of New England***.**

Epilogue

*I*n this Year of Our Lord 1992—276 years since the merchants and shipowners of Boston first built Boston Light—lighthouses and other aids to navigation still play an important role for seagoing men. But, quite fittingly, it is Boston Light that is the only manned lighthouse today. All others have been automated or discontinued, although in many cases Coast Guard families are occupying the keepers' houses, as at Highland Light in North Truro.

The move toward automation is undoubtedly more efficient and cost-effective for the Coast Guard, which is always struggling to "make do" with increased duties such as drug interdiction on the high seas. But something precious has been lost in the process: the *human* component provided by the dedication and attention to duty of the keepers and their wives. They lived, often for many years, a hard—often extremely lonely—life under conditions which we today would consider abysmally bad. One wonders how, for example, a family with fourteen children could have survived in the tiny, uncomfortable, damp boxes of dwellings that were the rule rather than the exception.

One such station did not receive running water or electricity until 1952—and that as the result of an appeal by the keeper's wife direct to President Truman.

These structures deserve protection for the part they have played in our history—and they are attracting growing interest on the part of a great many groups across the country who have raised money and donated time and effort to their preservation. Many are in private hands and have been lovingly refurbished and opened to the public. For instance, the Gurnet Lighthouse in Plymouth, Massachusetts, is operated and manned by the Massachusetts chapter of the United States Lighthouse Society. And the Truro Historical Society is working to raise funds to save historic Highland Light (1797) from destruction through erosion of the 133-foot-high cliff on which it stands.

Readers who live in "lighthouse country" or elsewhere may well want to look up their local lighthouse group and participate in the rewarding work of preserving these priceless relics of our maritime history. Or they may want to join one of the large national organizations. Here are five:

American Lighthouse Historical Society
Box 50186, Jacksonville Beach, FL 32250

Great Lakes Lighthouse Keepers Association
Box 580, Allen Park, MI 48101

Lighthouse Preservation Society
Box 736, Rockport, MA 01966

The Shore Village Museum
104 Limerock Street, Rockland, ME 04841

The United States Lighthouse Society
244 Kearny Street—Fifth Floor
San Francisco, CA 94108

Some lighthouses in private hands have become bed-and-breakfast inns, where guests may experience living at a lighthouse station. And all of the Cape and Island lighthouses discussed here (except Great Point on Nantucket, a replica) are in the National Register of Historic Places.

And so, as I watch from my house the sweep of Highland Light across the sky, I bless the makers and keepers of the lights for their hard-bitten dedication to duty over the long years.

Excerpts from

Instructions to Light-Keepers of the United States

(Senate Document 22),
Lighthouse Board, 1852

No. 3.

Instructions for light-keepers of the United States.

STATIONS WITH TWO OR MORE KEEPERS.

1. The lamps shall be lighted punctually every day at sunset, and extinguished at sunrise.

2. The lamps shall be kept burning bright and clear every night from sunset to sunrise; and in order that the greatest degree of light may be uniformly maintained, the wicks must be trimmed every four hours, or oftener if necessary, and clean glass chimneys fitted on; and special care must be taken to cut the tops of the wicks exactly even, to produce a flame of uniform shape, free from smoky points.

3. The light-keepers shall keep a regular and constant watch in the light-room throughout the night; the first watch to commence at sunset. The light-keepers are to take the watches alternately, in such manner that he who has the first watch one night shall have the second watch the next night. The length or duration of the watch shall not, in ordinary cases, exceed four hours; but during the period between the months of September and March, (both inclusive,) the first watch shall change at eight o'clock. The watches shall at all times be so arranged as to have a change at midnight.

4. The principal keeper will be particular to note on his journal the time at which all lights usually visible from the lantern of his tower are lighted up; he will also specify the hour of the disappearance of any of them, and note at such times the condition of the weather and atmosphere.

5. At stations where there is only one light-room, the daily duty shall be laid out in two departments, and the light-keepers shall change from one department to the other every Sunday night.

First department.—The light-keeper who has this department shall, immediately after the morning watch, cleanse and polish the reflectors or refractors; he shall also thoroughly cleanse the lamps and carefully dust the chandelier. He shall supply the burners with wicks, the lamps with oil, and shall have everything connected with the apparatus in a state of readiness for lighting up in the evening.

Second department.—The light-keeper who has this department shall cleanse the glass of the lantern, lamp-glasses, copper and brass work, and utensils, the walls, floors, and balcony of the light-room, and the apparatus and machinery therewith connected, together with the tower stairs, passage, doors, and windows, from the light-room to the oil-cellar.

6. For the more effectual cleansing of the glass of the lantern, and management of the lamps at the time of lighting, both light-keepers shall be upon watch throughout the first hour of the first watch every night during the winter period, between the first day of September and the last day of March, when they shall jointly do the duty of the light-room during that hour. These changes to and from the double watch must be noted by the keepers in the monthly returns for September and April. The light-keepers must return to the light-house on all occasions, so as to be in time to attend the double watch at lighting time during the period above specified.

7. At those stations where there are two light-rooms and two keepers, each light-keeper shall perform the entire duty of both departments in the light-room to which he may be specially assigned. But after the first hour of the first watch, the light-keeper who has charge of this watch shall perform the whole duty of trimming and attending the lights of both light-rooms till the expiration of his watch; and, in like manner, his successor in the watch shall perform the whole duty of both light-rooms during his watch.

8. At stations where there are a number of lights requiring more than two keepers, the duties shall, in the absence of special instructions, be apportioned in such manner as to equalize, as nearly as possible, the duties of all the keepers.

9. No light-keeper shall be exempted from keeping a regular watch, and performing a full share of duty, except for sickness; in which case the fact must be entered on the journal, and reported to the district inspector without delay.

10. The plate-glass must be cleaned within and without, by night as well as by day, particularly from the drift snow and sleet, and the moisture which is liable to accumulate in the interior of the lantern.

11. The light-keeper on duty shall on no pretence whatever, during his watch, leave the light-room and balcony, except to call his relief, and at stations where there are two or more lights which require his visits during the watch.

12. The principal keepers of revolving lights are required to give their particular attention to the MOVABLE MACHINERY; to see that it is well cleaned in every part, and kept free from dust; well oiled with clockmakers' oil; uniform in its motions, without unnecessary friction of its parts; performs its revolutions regularly within the prescribed period of time; wound up at the expiration of regular intervals of time; the motive-weight rests during the day upon a support to relieve the machinery and cord; and that the CORD is not in danger of parting from long use.

13. When the frame on which the lamps and reflectors are placed is movable, care must be taken to place the lights in the same position every night, leaving the dark side towards that portion of the horizon which does not require to be lighted; and the reflectors and lamps must be kept firmly screwed to the frame, with the lips of the reflectors perpendicular to the horizon, except in cases where it is specially required that they should be slightly inclined.

14. Strict attention must be given to the ventilation of the lantern, taking care to keep the leeward ventilators sufficiently open to admit the requisite quantity of air to produce steady, clear, and bright lights.

15. The principal light-keeper is held responsible for the safety and good order of the stores, utensils, and apparatus of every description, and for everything being put to its proper use, and kept in its proper place. He shall take care that none of the stores or materials are wasted, and shall observe the strictest economy and the most careful management, yet so as to maintain, in every respect, the best possible light.

16. The principal light-keeper shall daily serve out the allowance of oil and other stores for the use of the light-room. The oil is to be measured by the assistant in sight of the principal light-keeper. The light-keepers are on no account to leave the turning-keys attached to the cranes of the oil-cisterns after drawing oil, but shall remove and deposite them on the tray beside the oil-measures, or hang them up in some safe and convenient place.

17. The light-keepers shall keep a daily journal of the quantity of oil expended, the routine of duty, and state of the weather, embodying any events of interest or importance relating to his duties that may occur. These shall be written in the journal-books to be kept at each station for the purpose, at the periods of the day when they occur, as they must on no account be trusted to memory. At the end of each quarter they shall make up and transmit to the district inspectors, under cover to the collector of the district, who is superintendent of lights, a return, which shall be an accurate copy of the journal for the preceding quarter.

18. The light-keepers are also required to take notice of any ship-wrecks which shall happen within the vicinity of the light-house, and to enter an account thereof, according to the prescribed form, in a book furnished to each station for this purpose; and in such account they shall state, if practicable, whether the light was seen by any on board the shipwrecked vessel, and recognised by them, and how long it was seen before the vessel struck. A copy of this entry shall form the ship-wreck return, and be forthwith forwarded to the inspector.

19. A book containing a note of the vessels passing each light-house shall be kept, and an annual schedule, showing the number of vessels in each month, shall be sent to the district inspector.

20. The quarterly and shipwreck returns are to be written by the assistant, and the accompanying letters by the principal keeper. The whole shall be carefully compared, and the addition of the columns tested by both light-keepers, who shall also sign the same as correct, according to the printed form; and the principal keeper shall transmit the same to the district inspector as prescribed, without unnecessary delay.

21. The principal light-keeper is held responsible for the regularity of the watches throughout the night, for the cleanliness and good order of the reflecting or refracting apparatus, machinery, and utensils, and for the due performance of the whole duty of the light-room or light-rooms, as the case may be, whether performed by him personally or by the assistant.

22. The principal light-keeper is also held responsible for the good order and condition of everything belonging to the light-house estab-lishment at the station under his charge, including the cleanliness of the apartments, passages, stairs, roofs, water-cisterns, wells, storerooms, workshops, privies, stables, ash-pits of the dwelling-houses, &c., &c.

23. The principal and assistant shall take especial care, at all times, that neither lucifer matches, nor anything else which is easily ignited, lighted lamps, candles, or fires, be left anywhere in the premises, so as to endanger the public property by fire. The fire-buckets are to be kept in the most convenient place for use, and, when the weather will

permit, filled with water ready for use, and they are on no account to be used for household purposes.

24. The light-keepers shall, under no circumstances, use tripoli powder for cleaning the refractors, or silvered parts of the reflectors, nor any other cleaning materials than the rouge, whiting, buffskins, and cleaning-cloths, &c., furnished by direction of the Light-house Board, and for the purposes designated in the directions to light-keepers.

25. Each package or parcel of rouge and whiting must be examined by the keeper before using it, by rubbing between his fingers, to ascertain that it is free from grit and other impurities; and should it be found to be of bad quality, and calculated to injure the apparatus, it must not be used. The tripoli powder shall be employed exclusively for cleaning the backs of the reflectors, and other brass work of the apparatus.

26. The light-keepers shall endeavor to keep in good order and repair the dikes enclosing the light-house grounds, the landing-places and roads leading from thence to the light-house, and the drains therewith connected, together with all other things placed under their charge.

27. When stores of any kind are to be landed for the use of the light-house, the light-keepers shall attend and give their assistance. The principal light-keeper must, upon these occasions, satisfy himself, as far as possible, of the quantity and condition of the stores received, which must be duly entered in the store-books and quarterly-return book.

28. The light-keepers are to make a report of the quality of the stores in the quarterly return for the quarter immediately succeeding their receipt, and earlier should circumstances render it necessary, and also for the fourth quarter annually; and this report must proceed upon special trial of the several cisterns of oil, and the other stores in detail, both at the time of receiving them and after the experience of sufficient time to test them fully.

29. Should the supply of light-house stores at any time appear to the principal light-keeper to be getting short, so as thereby to endanger the regular appearance of the light, he shall immediately inform the district inspector, and, by prudent management of the lights, guard against a total consumption of the supplies before others can be received.

30. The light-keepers are prohibited from carrying on any trade or business whatever which will take them from the premises, or in any other manner cause the neglect of their public duties.

31. The light-keepers have permission to go from home to draw their salaries, and also to attend public worship on Sunday, but on no other occasion without the permission of the district inspector. The assistant light-keepers, on all occasions of leave of absence, must consult the principal light-keeper as to the proper time for such leave, and obtain his consent; in like manner, the principal light keeper shall duly intimate his intention of going from home to the assistant light-keeper; it being expressly ordered that only one light-keeper shall be absent from the light-house at one and the same time.

32. While the principal light-keeper is absent, or is incapacited for duty by sickness, the full charge of the light-room duty and of the premises shall devolve upon the assistant, who shall, in that case, have ac-

cess to the keys of the light-room stores, and be held responsible in all respects as the principal light-keeper.

33. The light-keepers are required to be sober and industrious, and orderly in their families. They are expected to be polite to strangers, in showing the premises at such hours as do not interfere with the proper duties of their office; it being expressly understood that strangers shall not be admitted to the light-room after sunset. Not more than three persons shall have access to the light-room at one and the same time during the day, and no stranger visiting the light-house shall be permitted to handle any part of the machinery or apparatus. The light-keepers must not, on any pretext, admit persons in a state of intoxication into the light-house.

34. The principal light-keeper is prohibited from selling any malt or spirituous liquors, and from allowing any to be sold on the premises under his charge.

35. In the event of any neglect of duty on the part of any light-keeper, the other light-keeper or light-keepers at the station shall give immediate notice of the circumstance to the district inspector, the party offending being permitted to send with the notice or report any explanations he may desire to make.

36. The light-keepers are to observe that the above general regulations are without prejudice to any more special instructions which may be made applicable to any particular light-house, or to such orders as may, from time to time, be issued by the Light-house Board.

37. All official communications for the Light-house Board must be transmitted through the district inspector, except in cases of emergency, when they may be sent direct to one of the secretaries of the Light-house Board, under cover to the honorable Secretary of the Treasury.

38. These instructions are to be hung up in a conspicuous place in the light-houses, and in the dwelling of the keepers, and the keepers and assistants are required to make themselves perfectly acquainted with them.

The breach of any of the foregoing instructions will subject the offending light-keepers to the serious displeasure of the department, and, in the absence of extenuating circumstances, to dismissal.

By order of the Light-house Board:

W. B. SHUBRICK,
Chairman.

THORNTON A. JENKINS, } *Secretaries.*
EDMUND L. F. HARDCASTLE, }

TREASURY DEPARTMENT,
Office Light-house Board, Washington city, October 14, 1852.

Approved:

THO. CORWIN,
Secretary of the Treasury.

Instructions for light-keepers of the United States.

LIGHT STATIONS WITH ONE KEEPER.

1. The lamps shall be lighted punctually every day at sunset, and extinguished at sunrise.

2. The lamps shall be kept burning bright and clear every night from sunset to sunrise; and in order that the greatest degree of light may be uniformly maintained, the wicks must be trimmed every four hours, or oftener if necessary, and clean glass chimneys fitted on; and special care must be taken to cut the tops of the wicks exactly even, to produce a flame of uniform shape, free from smoky points.

3. The keeper is held responsible for the careful watching and trimming of the light throughout the night, and is expected to be in attendance during the day, never absenting himself from duty without permission from the district inspector, except in the cases hereinafter provided for, in which cases he must furnish an efficient substitute. Any negligence will subject him to the severest displeasure of the department.

4. The keeper will be particular to note in his journal the time at which all lights usually visible from the lantern of his tower are lighted up. He will also specify the hour of the disappearance of any of them, and note, at such times, the condition of the weather and atmosphere.

5. The plate-glass must be cleaned within and without, by night as well as by day, particularly of the drift snow, sleet, and the moisture which is liable to accumulate in the interior of the lantern; and must polish and clean the reflectors, or refractors, and lamps, trim the lamps, and put the light-room in perfect order, by 10 o'clock a. m. daily, and be very particular with the order and cleanliness of the buildings, apartments, and premises.

6. Strict attention must be given to the ventilation of the lantern, taking care to keep the leeward ventilators sufficiently open to admit the requisite quantity of air to produce steady, clear, and bright lights.

7. The keepers of revolving lights are required to give their particular attention to the MOVABLE MACHINERY; to see that it is well cleaned in every part, and kept free from dust; well oiled with clockmakers' oil; uniform in its motions, without unnecessary friction of its parts; performs its revolutions regularly within the prescribed period of time; wound up at the expiration of regular intervals of time; the motive-weight rests during the day upon a support, to relieve the machinery and cord; and that the CORD is not in danger of parting from long use.

8. When the frame upon which the lamps and reflectors are placed is movable, care must be taken to place the lights in the same position every night, leaving the dark side towards that portion of the horizon which does not require to be lighted; and the reflectors and lamps must be kept firmly screwed to the frame, with the lips of the reflectors perpendicular to the horizon, except in cases where it is specially required that they should be slightly inclined.

9. The keeper is held responsible for the safety and good order of the stores, utensils, and apparatus of every description, and for everything being put to its proper use and kept in its proper place. He

shall take care that none of the stores or materials are wasted, and shall observe the strictest economy and the most careful management, yet so as to maintain, in every respect, the best possible light.

10. He is on no account to leave the turning-keys attached to the cranes of the oil-cisterns after drawing oil, but shall remove and deposite them on the tray beside the oil-measures, or hang them up in some safe and convenient place.

11. He shall keep a daily journal of the quantity of oil expended, and state of the weather, embodying any events of interest or importance that may occur. These shall be written in the journal-books to be kept at each station for the purpose, at the periods of the day when they occur, as they must on no account be trusted to memory. At the end of each quarter, he shall make up and transmit to the district inspectors, under cover to the collector of the district, who is superintendent of lights, a return, which shall be an accurate copy of the journal for the preceding quarter.

12. He is also required to take notice of any shipwrecks which shall happen within the vicinity of the light-house, and to enter an account thereof, according to the prescribed form, in a book furnished to each station for this purpose; and in such account he shall state, if practicable, whether the light was seen by any one on board the shipwrecked vessel, and recognised by him, and how long it was seen before the vessel struck. A copy of this entry shall form the shipwreck return, and be forthwith forwarded to the inspector.

13. A book containing a note of the vessels passing each light-house shall be kept; and an annual schedule, showing the number of vessels in each quarter, shall be sent to the district inspector.

14. The light-keeper is also held responsible for the good order and condition of everything belonging to the light-house establishment at the station under his charge, including the cleanliness of the apartments, passages, stairs, roofs, water-cisterns, wells, storerooms, workshops, privies, stables, ash-pits of the dwelling-houses, &c., &c.

15. The light-keeper shall take especial care, at all times, that neither lucifer matches, nor anything else which is easily ignited, lighted lamps, candles, or fires, be left anywhere in the premises, so as to endanger the public property by fire. The fire-buckets are to be kept in the most convenient place for use, and, when the weather will permit, filled with water ready, and they are on no account to be removed for household purposes.

16. The light-keeper shall, under no circumstances, use tripoli power for cleaning the refractors, or silvered parts of the reflectors, nor any other cleaning materials than the rouge, whiting, buffskins, and cleaning-cloths, &c., furnished by direction of the Light-house Board, and for the purposes designated in the directions to light-keepers. Each package or parcel of rouge and whiting must be examined by the keeper before using it, by rubbing between his fingers, to ascertain that it is free from grit and other impurities, and, should it be found to be of bad quality, and calculated to injure the apparatus, it must not be used. The tripoli powder shall be used exclusively for cleaning the backs of the reflectors, and other brass work of the apparatus.

17. The light-keeper shall endeavor to keep in good order and re-

pair the dikes enclosing the light-house grounds, the landing-places and roads leading from thence to the light-house, and the drains therewith connected, together with all other things placed under his charge.

18. When stores of any kind are to be landed for the use of the light-house, the keeper shall attend and give his assistance. He shall satisfy himself, upon these occasions, as far as possible, of the quantity and condition of the stores received, which must be duly entered in the store-books and quarterly-return book.

19. The light-keeper is to make a report of the quality of the stores, in the return for the quarter immediately succeeding their receipt, and earlier should circumstances render it necessary, and also for the fourth quarter annually; and this report must proceed upon special trial of the several cisterns of oil, and the other stores in detail, both at the time of receiving them and after the expiration of sufficient time to test them fully.

20. Should the supply of light-house stores at any time appear to the keeper to be getting short, so as thereby to endanger the regular appearance of the light, he shall immediately inform the district inspector, and, by prudence in the management of the lights, guard against a total consumption of the supplies before others can be received.

21. The light-keeper is prohibited from carrying on any trade or business whatever, which will take him from the premises, or in any other manner cause the neglect of his public duties.

22. He has permission to go from home to draw his salary, and also to attend public worship on Sunday, but on no other occasion without the permission of the district inspector. In case of sickness he must provide a temporary keeper, and report the fact, without delay, to the district inspector or superintendent of lights.

23. The light-keeper is required to be sober and industrious, and orderly in his family. He is expected to be polite to strangers, in showing the premises at such hours as do not interfere with the proper duties of his office; it being expressly understood that strangers shall not be admitted to the light-room after sunset. Not more than three persons shall have access to the light-room at one and the same time during the day, and no stranger visiting the light-house shall be permitted to handle any part of the machinery or apparatus. The light-keeper must not, on any pretext, admit persons in a state of intoxication into the light-house. He is prohibited from selling any malt or spirituous liquors, and from allowing any to be sold on the premises under his charge.

24. The light-keeper is to observe that the above general regulations are without prejudice to any more special instructions which may be made applicable to any particular light-house, or to such orders as may, from time to time, be issued by the Light-house Board.

25. All official communications for the Light-house Board must be transmitted through the district inspector, except in cases of emergency, when they may be sent direct to one of the secretaries of the Light-house Board, under cover, to the honorable Secretary of the Treasury.

26. These instructions are to be hung up in a conspicuous place in the light-house, and in the keeper's dwelling. The keeper is required to make himself perfectly acquainted with them.

The breach of any of the foregoing instructions will subject the offending light-keeper to the severest displeasure of the department, and, in the absence of extenuating circumstances, to dismissal.

By order of the Light-house Board:

W. B. SHUBRICK,
Chairman.

THORNTON A. JENKINS, ⎱
EDMUND L. F. HARDCASTLE, ⎰ *Secretaries.*

TREASURY DEPARTMENT,
Office Light-house Board, Washington city, October 14, 1852.

Approved:

THO. CORWIN,
Secretary of the Treasury.

Excerpt from
Lights of the United States,
Lighthouse Board, 1854

Number.	Name.	Location.	Latitude north.	Longitude west.	Number of lights and relative positions.	Fog signal.
54	Plymouth.............	On Gurnet Point, north side of entrance to Plymouth harbor, Mass.	42 00 12	70 35 42	2 31 feet apart, NW. & SE.	....
55	Race Point.............	Northwesterly point of Cape Cod, Mass.	42 03 42	70 14 16	1	....
56	Long Point	On Long Point shoal, southwest entrance to Provincetown harbor, Mass.	42 02 00	70 09 48	1	....
-57	Parmet Harbor.........	On the north part of Parmet harbor, south end of Salt Works.	....	....	1	....
58	Mayo's Beach	At the head of Wellfleet bay..	41 55 48	70 01 42	1	••••
59	Billingsgate............	West side of entrance to Wellfleet, Mass.	41 51 36	70 03 54	1	....
60	Sandy Neck............	West side of entrance to Barnstable, Mass.	41 43 18	70 16 30	1	....
61	CAPE COD, (Highlands, TRURO.)	On the seaward side of Cape Cod, (Highlands,) Truro, Mass.	D. M. S. 42 02 24	D. M. S. 70 03 18	1	....
62	Nauset Beach, (beacons.)	At Eastham, on the east side of Cape Cod, Mass.	41 51 40	69 56 42	3 150 ft. apart, N. and S.	....
63	Chatham	On the main, west side of Chatham harbor, Mass., and Nauset beach being on the east side.	41 40 16	69 56 36	2 70 feet apart, N. and S.	....
64	Monomoy Point........	On Cape Malabar, the southern extremity of Cape Cod, Mass.	41 33 30	69 59 18	1	....
65	Succonessett Shoal light-vessel.	....	....	....	1	Bell....
66	Killpond Bar light-vessel.	....	....	....	1	Bell....
67	Pollock Rip light-vessel..	Off Chatham, 4 miles east ½ south from Monomoy lighthouse.	....	....	1	Bell....
68	Shovelfull Shoals light-vessel.	Off Chatham, 2½ miles south-southwest ¼ west from Monomoy Point light-house.	....	....	1	Bell....
69	NANTUCKET, (Great Point.)	On Sandy or Great Point, the northeast extremity of Nantucket island.	41 23 24	70 02 25	1	....

Number.	Fixed or revolving, &c.	Interval of revolution or flash.	Distance visible in nautical miles.	Color of tower or vessel.	Height of tower from base to centre of lantern.	Height of light above sea level.	Size of lens.	Size of reflectors.	Number of lamps.	When built.	When light refitted.	Remarks.
54	2 fixed...	......	15	White.....	33	93	......	16 / 16	8 / 8	1769	1813	Two octagonal wooden towers—serve as a range to clear Brown's bank coming from the southward and eastward.
55	Revolv'g.	1 30	11	White.....	28	35	......	15	10	1816	1845	Rubble-stone tower topped with brick—serves as a guide to enter Cape Cod bay.
56	Fixed ...	......	11	Black	25	28	......	15	10	1826	1850	Lantern on keeper's house, for local purposes, is seen from Woodend bar, and illuminates nearly the entire horizon into the harbor.
57	Fix'd, red	......	6	White.....	26	31?	......	21	1	1849	.....	Light on keeper's house; tide harbor for small vessels.
58	Fixed ...	......	6	Red........	25	26	......	14	3	1838	.....	Harbor-light on keeper's dwelling.
59	Fixed ...	......	12	White. ...	26	40	......	13	8	1822	1848	Light on keeper's dwelling; local light for Wellfleet, Orleans, and Eastham.
60	Fixed ...	......	11	White	28	33	......	21	4	1836	1850	Harbor light on keeper's
61	Fixed ...	M. S.	20	White	36	171	Order.	Inch. 21	15	1797	1840	Brick tower; lantern straw color; 43 miles from Cape Ann lights, 45 miles from Sankaty Head light, and 41 miles from Boston light.
62	3 fixed...	......	15	White	18	93	......	14 / 14 / 14	6 / 6 / 6	1837	.....	Three circular brick towers, whitewashed; lanterns black. Abreast of these lights the tides divide and run in opposite directions.
63	2 fixed...	......	14	White	40 / 40	70 / 70	......	14 / 14	9 / 9	1808	1841	Two circular towers; lanterns black.
64	Fixed ...	......	11	Red........	30	33	......	14	8	1823	1849	Cast-iron tower; lantern white, with black dome. This and the Chatham lights serve to guide vessels in going through the north channel on the south side of the Cape, passing north of the Handkerchief, and Bishop, and Clerk's.
65	Fixed ...	......	.....	....	....	......	......	12	8	1854	.....	Building.
66	Fixed ...	......	.....	....	....	......	......	12	8	1854	.....	Building.
67	Fixed ...	......	12	Red........	30	45	......	None.	1	1849	. ...	Fog-bell: day-mark, one red ball at the mast-head. A north by east ¼ east course (mag.) from near this vessel, if made good, will clear the shoals. The black buoy, distant half mile north by east from the vessel, must be left on the porthand.
68	Fixed ...	......	11	Green......	28	40	......	None.	1	1852	.....	Fog-bell: day-mark, one green ball at mast-head. This vessel lies west from Pollock Rip light-vessel. There is a black buoy near this vessel, on the point of the Shovelfull shoal.
69	Fixed ...	......	14	White.....	60	70	......	21	15	1769	1817 1845	Stone tower—lantern black.

Number.	Name.	Location.	Latitude north.	Longitude west.	Number of lights and relative positions.	Fog signal.
70	SANKATY HEAD....	On the southeast extremity of the island of Nantucket, about south by west, 23 miles from Pollock Rip light-vessel.	41 16 59	69 57 35	1	....
71	*Nantucket New South Shoals light-vessel.*	Placed about two miles south of the southern extremity of the new shoal of Nantucket in 14 fathoms water.	40 56 30	69 51 30	2	Bell & guns.
72	GAY HEAD..........	On the western extremity of Martha's Vineyard island.	*D. M. S.* 41 20 52	*D. M. S.* 70 49 48	1	....
	VINEYARD SOUND, MASS.					
73	Point Gammon........	South side of Cape Cod, on the eastern side of entrance to Hyannis harbor, Mass.	41 36 33	70 15 39	1	....
74	Hyannis	Harbor light on the main, inside of the Breakwater, Massachusetts.	41 38 00	70 18 00	1	....
75	*Cross Rip light-vessel...*	Northwest of Nantucket, off Tuckanuck shoal, Mass.	41 26 44	70 17 05	1	Bell...
76	Nantucket Cliff beacons.	On the beach, north of Nantucket harbor, Mass.	....	....	2 300 ft. apart, NW. & SE.	....
77	Brant Point..........	On Brant Point, entrance to Nantucket harbor, Mass.	41 17 24	70 05 12	1	....
78	Nantucket beacon......	South side of Nantucket harbor, Mass.	41 16 24	70 04 24	1	....

Number.	Fixed or revolving, &c.	Interval of revolution or flash.	Distance visible in nautical miles.	Color of tower or vessel.	Height of tower from base to centre of lantern.	Height of light above sea level.	Size of lens.	Size of reflectors.	Number of lamps.	When built.	When light refitted.	Remarks.
70	F. V. F.	1 00	20	White, red & white.	65	150	[⊙ 2]	.....	1	1849	....	This light shows a brilliant flash of ten seconds' duration once in every minute, and a fixed light during the remaining 50 seconds within the range of visibility of the fixed light. Cape Cod light, 47 miles; and Gay Head light, 39 miles distant from this light
71	2 fixed...	......	12	Red........	....	44	......	12 12	8 8	1854	....	Magnetic bearings from light-vessel to centre Old South shoal north by east, distant 8 miles; to Tom Never's Head, north 26° west, distant 21 miles; to Block Island lights, west-north-west, distance 78 miles; to Sandy Hook light-vessel, west, distant 180 miles. Fog-signal bell, and when necessary sig
72	Revolv'g.	M. S. 1 30	20	White.....	35	191	Order.	Inch. 21	14	1799	1842 1854	Octagonal wooden tower—lantern white. A guide to Vineyard's sound and Buzzard's bay, 39 miles from Sankaty Head light; 48 miles from Montauk Point light, and 30 miles from Point Judith. A rocky shoal, distant 1½ mile, lies northwest from this light. Cuttyhunk island bears north 45° west, distant 7½ miles.
73	Fixed ...	......	13	White.....	20	70	......	14	11	1816	1843	Whitewashed stone tower—lantern painted black. The "Bishop and Clerk's" (spindle) lies south by east, and a sunken rock lies south, 1 mile, from this light.
74	Fixed ...	......	8	White.....	16	36	......	14	3	1849	....	Leading light for Hyannis Harbor—on the main land north 5° east, (mag.) from the east end of the breakwater.
75	Fixed ...	......	7	Straw color with red streak.	....	39	......	None.	1	1828	....	This vessel lies in 8 fathoms water—has a fog-bell; a black buoy, 200 fathoms distant, bearing southwest ¼ south, (mag.) lies in 11 feet water.
76	2 fixed ..	......	4	White.....	....	8 10	......	......	1 1	1838	....	These are two small pyramidal wooden structures northwest by west ¼ west (mag.) from Brant Point light. They range with the outer buoy of the western entrance.
77	Fixed ...	......	11	White.....	37	43	......	14	9	1794	1849	Wooden tower. This tower, in range with Nantucket beacon on the south side of the harbor, will clear Black flat, leaving the shoal on the starboard hand.
78	Fixed ...	......	5	White.....	....	10	24	......	1	1820	1825	A small wooden house—the light shown from a window.

Number.	Name.	Location.	Latitude north.	Longitude west.	Number of lights and relative positions.	Fog-signal.
79	Cape Poge.............	Northeast point of Martha's Vineyard.	41 25 14	70 26 44	1...............	....
80	Edgartown.............	Entrance to Edgartown harbor.	41 23 24	70 29 48	1...............	....
81	Holmes's Hole, (West Chop.)	On West Chop, western entrance to Holmes's Hole harbor, Mass.	41 28 54	70 35 50	1...............	....
82	Holmes's Hole beacons.	At Holmes's Hole harbor, ranging with the two channels to the anchorage.	....	....	3...............	....
83	Nobsque Point....	East-southeast of entrance to Wood's Hole harbor, Mass.	41 30 54	70 39 00	1...............	....
84	Tarpaulin Cove.......	West side of the Cove on Naushon island, Mass.	41 28 07	70 45 06	1...............	....
85	*Vineyard Sound light-vessel.*	Near the rocks called "Sow and Pigs."	D. M. S.	D. M. S.	2...............	Bell...
	BUZZARD'S BAY, MASS.					
86	Cuttyhunk.............	On the southwest point of Cuttyhunk island, entrance to Buzzard's bay.	41 24 48	70 56 42	1...............	....
87	Dumpling Rock	Off Round Hill, south-southwest of Clark's Point light and New Bedford, Mass.	41 32 18	70 55 36	1...............	....
88	Clark's Point	West side of entrance to New Bedford harbor, Mass.	41 35 30	70 54 12	1...............	....
89	Palmer's Island........	On northeast extremity of the island in New Bedford, Mass.	41 37 36	70 54 12	1...............	....
90	Ned's Point.............	Near Mattapoisett harbor, east of New Bedford.	41 39 00	70 47 24	1...............	....
91	Bird Island.............	East side of entrance to Sippican harbor.	41 40 06	70 42 40	1...............	....
92	Wing's Neck..........	At the head of Buzzard's bay, in Sandwich.	....	....	1	....
93	*Brenton's Reef light-vessel.*	Off east entrance to Newport, R. I.	....	....	2...............	Bell...

Number.	Fixed or revolving, &c.	Interval of revolution or flash.	Distance visible in nautical miles.	Color of tower or vessel.	Height of tower from base to centre of lantern.	Height of light above sea level.	Size of lens.	Size of reflectors.	Number of lamps.	When built.	When light refitted.	Remarks.
79	Fixed ...	......	13	White......	35	55	......	14	11	1801	1845	Wooden tower whitewashed—lantern black. This light is seen at sea over the land.
80	Fixed ...	......	12	White......	22	37	......	14	9	1828	.....	Light on keeper's house.
81	Fixed ...	......	12	White......	33	60	......	15	9	1817	.....	
82	3 fixed...	......	....	....	....	....	[⊙ 6]	......	1 each	1854	.....	Building—ranges for entering the harbor at Holmes's Hole.
83	Fixed ...	......	13	White......	29	80	......	15	10	1828	.....	Light on keeper's dwelling; lantern black; leading mark in running through the Vineyard sound.
84	Fixed ...	......	13	White......	32	80	......	15	9	1817	.....	This light is seen from Gay Head, and bears northeast by north, (mag.)
85	2 fixed...	M. S.	7	Red, with straw-color streak.	....	34 23	Order.	Inch. None.	2	......	......	Fog-bell: day marks, two balls color of the vessel. Cuttyhunk light bears northeast ¼ east, Gay Head light southeast by east, and Dumpling light north-northeast. A dangerous rock lies on the range between the vessel and Dumpling light.
86	Fixed ...	......	12	White......	32	42	......	15	9	1823	.....	Brick and stone tower: lantern black. In entering Buzzard's bay, bring the light to bear east distant three miles, and then steer northeast by north.
87	Fixed ...	......	12	White......	33	42	......	15	10	1828	.....	Light on keeper's dwelling. Clark's Point light bears north-northeast.
88	Fixed ...	......	12	White......	48	57	......	16	9	1800	....	Cuttyhunk light bears south 20° west, distant 11 miles.
89	Fixed ...	......	9	White......	28	32	......	14	8	1849	.....	Lantern white.
90	Fixed ...	......	11	White......	32	43	......	14	8	1847	.....	Lantern black.
91	Revolv'g.	1.20	10	White......	29	35	......	14	10	1819	1852	Lantern black.
92	Fixed ...	......	10	White......	29	44	......	14	8	1849	.....	Light on keeper's house.
93	2 fixed...	......	12	Straw color	....	50 40	......	None	2	1853	.....	Moored in 13 fathoms water; painted straw color, with "Brenton's reef" in black letters on each quarter; fog-bell. Point Judith light bears southwest ¼ west; Beaver Tail, northwest; Castle Hill Point, north by east.

A Guided Automobile Tour of the Lighthouses of Cape Cod and the Islands

CAPE COD

Cross Sagamore Bridge (Rte. 3) onto Rte. 6. Almost at once take exit to Rte. 6A to Barnstable.

SANDY NECK LIGHTHOUSE, BARNSTABLE—(Inaccessible by road but visible across the harbor) In Barnstable Village turn left at the stop light onto Mill Way. Drive straight to the water. (Bring telephoto lens or binoculars.)

NAUSET LIGHTHOUSE, EASTHAM—Stay on 6A through Orleans center to Rte. 6. At the stop light (Seashore Center on right) turn right on Nauset Road. After about 1-1/2 miles turn right on Cable Road. "Three Sisters" and Nauset Lighthouse are at the end.

MAYO'S BEACH KEEPER'S HOUSE, WELLFLEET—From Cable Road turn right on Nauset Road; it rejoins Rte. 6. At the second stop light (in Wellfleet) turn left on Main Street and then left on Commercial Street to the harbor. Turn right on Kendrick Road about 1/4 mile to see the green keeper's house (privately owned).

HIGHLAND LIGHTHOUSE, NORTH TRURO—Return to Rte. 6. Go past Truro Center to North Truro. Follow signs to Highland Lighthouse, east of Rte. 6.

PROVINCETOWN LIGHTS—(All three—Long Point Wood End, and Race Point—are inaccessible by road. The best view is from seaward.) A good view of Race Point may be had by taking Race Point Road (at the stop light on Rte. 6) to its end. The other two may also be seen across the harbor from the end of Commercial Street (the main street) in Provincetown. (Telephoto lenses are needed.)

CHATHAM LIGHTHOUSE—Return to Rte. 6 to Orleans and take Rte. 28 to Chatham. At the rotary in the center turn left onto Main Street. Follow it to the end and turn right on Shore Road to the lighthouse and a fine view of the recent break in the outer beach opposite the light.

STAGE HARBOR LIGHTHOUSE, CHATHAM—(Inaccessible by road. Privately owned.)

MONOMOY POINT LIGHT, CHATHAM—(Inaccessible by road. The best view is from seaward.)

BASS RIVER LIGHTHOUSE, WEST DENNIS—Return to Rte. 28 west. Drive through Chatham, Harwich, and Dennisport. At the start of West Dennis shopping center turn left on School Street and left on Lower County Road. Turn right on Lighthouse Road to the sign for the Lighthouse Inn (a fine place for lunch or dinner too).

SOUTH HYANNIS LIGHTHOUSE—Return to Rte. 28 west. Drive through South Yarmouth and West Yarmouth (about four miles from the Bass River Bridge) and bear left on East Main Street at the traffic light. At the fourth traffic light on Main Street, turn left on Sea Street and drive to the parking lot at its end. Walk east on the beach and then out onto the breakwater most of the way. You will be able to see and photograph South Hyannis Lighthouse (privately owned). To your left across Hyannis harbor you can see Point Gammon Lighthouse (stone tower, privately owned), and south of it the Bishop and Clerks beacon where that lighthouse used to be. (Directions thanks to Dr. Richard Sommers)

NOBSKA LIGHTHOUSE, WOODS HOLE—Return to Rte. 28 west and drive to Falmouth. At the end of the village green turn left on Woods Hole Road. After about three miles turn left on Church Street to the lighthouse.

WING'S NECK LIGHTHOUSE, BOURNE (POCASSET)—Return to the Falmouth Green and take Rte. 28 north. After about 7/10 of a mile past the rotary and entrance to Otis Base, turn left on Barlow's Landing Road. After 2.2 miles turn right on Wing's Neck Road (which runs into Lighthouse Road), a total of 2.7 miles to the lighthouse property (privately owned). TELEPHOTO LENS IS NEEDED FOR PICTURES.

This completes the tour of Cape Cod's lighthouses. Return to Rte. 28 and turn left. This takes you to the Bourne Bridge rotary. Route I-495 starts just over the bridge.

MARTHA'S VINEYARD

Usually the ferry from Woods Hole arrives at Vineyard Haven. In summer occasionally one lands at Oak Bluffs. If so, drive to Vineyard Haven, since the tour and mileages start there. NOTE: *Zero your odometer.*

HOLMES'S HOLE (WEST CHOP LIGHTHOUSE)—Leaving the ferry, follow traffic to the stop sign. Turn right and then take the first right onto Main Street. Drive straight out Main Street two miles to the lighthouse.

GAY HEAD LIGHTHOUSE—Continue in the same direction. Across the Sound you can see Nobska Lighthouse in the distance. After 1/2 mile bear right on Franklin Street and continue straight. After 1.8 miles, turn right on Center (cemetery is on your left). Then turn left at the stop sign and bear right at the yield sign onto Pine Tree Road (leaving cemetery on your right).

Turn right at the stop sign onto State Road. Continue straight ahead through West Tisbury to Gay Head on State Road. At 10.2 miles turn right toward Menemsha (not Gay Head). At 15.9 miles turn left to Gay Head. At Beetlebung Corner (17 miles), turn right to Gay Head. At 21 miles on the right is the retirement home of Frank Grieder, keeper at Gay Head (1937–1948). Go through Gay Head, and at 23.2 miles is the lighthouse. Across the water to the right is Cuttyhunk Island.

EDGARTOWN LIGHTHOUSE—Return to Beetlebung Corner. Bear right and drive through West Tisbury. At 34.8 miles bear right to Edgartown. Continue straight ahead to a stop sign at 43 miles. Turn right, then left to Edgartown center. Turn right down Main Street .2 mile and turn left on North Water Street (a brick building is on your right) to the lighthouse.

A public walk runs alongside a house to Lighthouse Beach. Cape Poge Lighthouse (on Chappaquiddick Island) can be seen in the distance to your left.

CAPE POGE LIGHTHOUSE—Driving there requires a special permit and a fee from the Trustees of Reservations, and a four-wheel-drive vehicle. The best bet is to rent an outboard and go out to the point, beach the boat, and walk to the lighthouse.

EAST CHOP LIGHTHOUSE—From Lighthouse Beach continue on Water Street. Left on Thayer Street, left on Fuller, and right on Morse. At 44.5 miles turn left at the stop sign and head for Oak Bluffs. Then turn right at the stop sign on Main Street. At 45.5 miles bear right to Beach Road and Oak Bluffs, along Nantucket Sound. Cape Poge is visible. At 50.5 miles turn left at the wharf (Lake Avenue), then straight ahead. Just beyond the harbor turn right on Commercial Avenue and then along the shore to Telegraph Hill and East Chop Lighthouse.

Continue in the same direction. At the bottom of the hill you will see West Chop Lighthouse across the harbor and Nobska Lighthouse across the Sound in Woods Hole. Turn right on Temehigan Avenue and Beach Road to Vineyard Haven. Turn right on Water Street to the ferry landing, where you started—a total of 54.4 miles round trip.

NANTUCKET

Take the Woods Hole, Martha's Vineyard, and Nantucket ferry from South Street, Hyannis, to Steamboat Wharf, Nantucket, OR

Take the Hy-Line ferry from Ocean Street, Hyannis, to Straight Wharf, Nantucket.

GREAT POINT LIGHTHOUSE—Inaccessible by road, but highly visible. The best view is from seaward.

BRANT POINT LIGHTHOUSE—(1) From Steamboat Wharf go two blocks on Broad Street, and turn right on South Beach Street. After four blocks, turn right on Easton Street to its end.

(2) From Straight Wharf take Main Street. After two blocks, turn right on Easy Street to its end at Broad Street. Turn left. Take the next right, South Beach Street, and then Easton Street, as above.

SANKATY HEAD LIGHTHOUSE—Retrace your route to Broad Street and turn left, then right on Easy Street. After three blocks, turn right on Main Street. After about 1/4 mile, turn left on Orange Street. After about 1-1/2 miles, at the rotary take Milestone Road to Siasconset.

Drive seven miles across the island to Siasconset. Turn left on Broadway to Sankaty Avenue, then right on Baxter Avenue to the lighthouse.

To return to the ferry, come back on Baxter Avenue to the first right, then right again on Sankaty Avenue. It becomes Polpis Road, which you follow back to Milestone Road and the rotary.

(1) Take the first right (Lower Orange) at the rotary. Turn right at the end of the two-way traffic and drive to the end on Francis Street. Turn left on Washington, which becomes Candle Street. At the end of Candle, take Easy Street to Broad Street and Steamboat Wharf.

(2) Follow the directions in (1) above onto Candle Street. Then take Cambridge Street to Straight Wharf.

A Partial Bibliography

Banks, Charles Edward. *The History of Martha's Vineyard*. Edgartown, MA: Dukes County Historical Society, 1966.

Bosworth, Janet. "The Cuttyhunk Lighthouse." Monograph, 1985.

Clemensen, A. Berle *et al*. *Three Sisters Lighthouses*. Washington, D.C.: National Park Service, 1986.

Chubb, M. Penniman. *Cape Cod Lighthouses*. Privately printed.

Deyo, Simeon L. (ed.). *History of Barnstable County, Massachusetts*. New York: H.W. Blake and Company, 1890.

Emerson, Amelia Forbes. *Early History of Naushon Island*. Boston: Howland and Company, 1981.

———. *Naushon Data*. Concord, MA: Privately printed, 1963.

Freeman, Frederick. *The History of Cape Cod*, 2 vols. Boston: George C. Rand & Avery, 1858.

Holland, Francis Ross. *America's Lighthouses*. New York: Dover Publications, 1988.

Ireland, Thomas. "South Hyannis Light." Unpublished paper.

Kittredge, Henry C. *Cape Cod: Its People and Their History*. Boston: Houghton Mifflin Company, 1930.

Lewis, Winslow. *Description of the Light-houses on the Coast of the United States*. Boston: Thomas G. Bangs, 1817.

Macy, William F. *The Story of Old Nantucket*. Boston: Houghton Mifflin Company, 1928.

Massachusetts Historical Commission. "Lighthouse Information Forms." (for lighthouses recommended for the National Register of Historic places). Boston: various dates.

Morison, Samuel Eliot. *By Land and By Sea*. New York: Alfred A. Knopf, 1953.

———. *The Maritime History of Massachusetts, 1783–1860*. Boston: Houghton Mifflin, 1921.

Railton, Arthur. "Cape Poge Light: Remote and Lonely." Edgartown, MA: *The Dukes County Intelligencer*, November 1983, February 1984, and May 1984.

———. "Gay Head Light: The Island's First." Edgartown, MA: *The Dukes County Intelligencer*, April 1982.

———. "Gay Head Light Gets the Wondrous Fresnel." Edgartown, MA: *The Dukes County Intelligencer*, May 1982.

Rich, Shebnah. *Truro, Cape Cod, or Land Marks and Sea Marks*. Boston: D. Lothrop and Company, 1884.

Spooner, Nathaniel. *Gleanings from the Records of the Boston Marine Society*. Boston: Boston Marine Society, 1879.

Stackpole, Edouard. *Lifesaving Nantucket*. Nantucket Life Saving Museum, 1972.

Starbuck, Alexander. *The History of Nantucket*. Boston: C.E. Goodspeed, 1924.

Stevenson, D. Alan. *The World's Lighthouses Before 1820*. London: The Oxford University Press, 1959.

Stone, Robert. "A History of the Lighthouse Inn." Unpublished paper.

Trayser, Donald. *Barnstable: Three Centuries of a Cape Cod Town*. Hyannis, MA: F.B. and F.P. Goss, 1939.

United States Coast Guard. *Historical Records*. Washington: January, 1950.

———. *Historically Famous Lighthouses*. Washington: GPO, 1957.

————. *Light List*, vol. 1. Washington: GPO, 1988.

United States Department of the Interior. *National Registry of Historic Places Nomination Form*. Washington: National Park Service, 1987.

United States Lighthouse Board. *Annual Reports*. Washington: various years.

————. *Instructions to Light-Keepers and Masters of Light-House Vessels*. Allen Park, Michigan: Great Lakes Lighthouse Keepers Association, 1989.

————. *Lists of Lights of the United States*. Washington: various years.

————. *Lighthouse Keepers' Journals*. Washington: numerous light stations and years.

Wayman, Dorothy. *Suckanessett*. Falmouth, MA: The Falmouth Publishing Company, 1930.

Welch, Wally. *The Lighthouses of Massachusetts*. Apopka, FL: Lighthouse Publications, 1989.

Wheeler, Wayne. "The History of the Administration of the USLH Service," *The Keeper's Log*, Winter and Spring, 1989.

Index

(Compiled by Constance Connell)
(Beginning chapter page numbers are bold-faced)

The different varieties of Lights are designated by the following Characters:

———— Fixed White.

- - - - Fixed Red

+ + + Flashing White

* * * * Flashing Red

+———— Fixed White varied by White Flashes

*———— Fixed White varied by Red Flashes

**———— Fixed White varied by Red & White Flashes

* + * + Flashing Red and White

———— Double Lights

Lights being built

The arcs of illumination are indicated only for some of the principal lights. The others can be found in the Light House List.

East Duxbury

Plymouth

Duxbury Pier Lt.

Plymouth

Manom

Wing's Neck Lt.

Ned's Pt. Lt.

Bird I. Lt.

New Bedford
Palmer's I. Lt.

Clarks Pt. Lt.

Dumpling Rock Lt.

State Boundary

BUZZARD'S BAY

Nobsque Pt. Lt.

Holmes Hole Lt.

N.

Tarpaulin Cove Lt.

East Chop

Hen and Chicken Lt. Ship

VINEYARD SOUND

Cuttyhunk Lt.

Vineyard Sd. Lt. Ship

Martha's Vineyard

Edgartown Lt.

Gay Head Lt.

No Man's Land